FRENCH WORDLIST

T. Murray

Head of Modern Languages,
Edgecliff School, Staffordshire

CASSELL

Cassell Publishers Ltd
Artillery House
Artillery Row
London
SW1P 1RT

Copyright © Cassell Publishers Ltd 1989

First published 1989

ISBN 0-304-31621-0

**British Library Cataloguing in Publication
Data**
Murray, T.
    Cassell's French wordlist.
    1. French language. French & English
    dictionaries
    I. Title
    443′.21

Printed in Great Britain by Anchor Press Ltd,
Tiptree, Essex
Typeset in Century Schoolbook by Witwell Ltd

Dedication

To my wife Rhoda. Also to my children Catherine, Clare,
Michael and Elizabeth without whose 'assistance' the
compilation of this book would have been far easier!

To the Teacher, Pupil and Parent

All the GCSE boards have issued vocabulary lists on which they will base their exams. No questions may be asked which require knowledge of words not on the lists.

Unfortunately, no English translation is provided with these lists and this leaves teachers in a quandary as to how to exploit them. In fact, it has been the incessant demands from my pupils for a translation that has caused me to write this book.

This GCSE vocabulary book is based on the vocabulary lists provided by the GCSE exam boards. It has been structured to cover the vocabulary lists of each and every board and the requirements of Standard Grade. Very simple words, unlikely words and some words which are the same in English have been omitted.

We are now being forced to use a number of different books to cover the four skill areas of listening, speaking, reading and writing. Few (if any) have a comprehensive French/English and English/French vocabulary list. Few (if any) of the major course-books have such a list. I am sure that GCSE and Standard Grade students of all ages will find this book a valuable companion as it provides both.

Space has been provided for any additional words that you might like to insert. Words like 'match' have been contextualised so that you know whether you are referring to a football match or a match for lighting a fire.

There is a section at the front covering numbers, days, months, seasons, time and weather.

Bonne chance!

T. Murray
Head of Modern Languages, Edgecliff School, Staffordshire.

Numbers

Cardinal numbers

0	zéro
1	un/une
2	deux
3	trois
4	quatre
5	cinq
6	six
7	sept
8	huit
9	neuf
10	dix
11	onze
12	douze
13	treize
14	quatorze
15	quinze
16	seize
17	dix-sept
18	dix-huit

Les nombres

Les nombres (m) cardinaux

19	dix-neuf
20	vingt
21	vingt et un(e)
22	vingt-deux etc
30	trente
40	quarante
50	cinquante
60	soixante
70	soixante-dix
71	soixante et onze
80	quatre-vingts
81	quatre-vingt-un(e)
90	quatre-vingt-dix
91	quatre-vingt-onze
100	cent
101	cent un(e)
190	cent quatre-vingt-dix
200	deux cents
211	deux cent onze

Ordinal numbers

Les nombres (m) ordinaux

first	premier	eleventh	onzième
second	deuxième	twelfth	douzième
third	troisième	seventeenth	dix-septième
fourth	quatrième	eighteenth	dix-huitième
fifth	cinquième	nineteenth	dix-neuvième
sixth	sixième	twentieth	vingtième
seventh	septième	twenty-first	vingt et unième
eighth	huitième	fiftieth	cinquantième
ninth	neuvième	hundredth	centième
tenth	dixième		

The days of the week

Les jours (m) de la semaine

Monday	lundi	today	aujourd'hui
Tuesday	mardi	yesterday	hier
Wednesday	mercredi	tomorrow	demain
Thursday	jeudi	the day before yesterday	avant-hier
Friday	vendredi		
Saturday	samedi		

Sunday	dimanche	the day after tomorrow	après-demain

on Tuesday	mardi	*Note:*
on Fridays	le vendredi	(i) no capital letter
every Saturday	tous les samedis	for days of the week in French
in the morning	le matin	(ii) Monday is
in the afternoon	l'après-midi	generally regarded
in the evening	le soir	as the first day of
in the night	la nuit	the week

The months of the year   Les mois (*m*) de l'année

January	janvier	July	juillet
February	février	August	août
March	mars	September	septembre
April	avril	October	octobre
May	mai	November	novembre
June	juin	December	décembre

What is the date today?

Quelle est la date aujourd' hui?

(It's) Monday the 13th of January (1992)

(C'est) le lundi treize (13) janvier (mille neuf cent quatre-vingt-douze *or* dix-neuf cent quatre-vingt-douze)

Sunday the 1st of May

Le dimanche premier (1er) mai

Note: no capital letter for months in French

The seasons   Les saisons (*f*)

spring	le printemps
summer	l'été (*m*)
autumn	l'automne (*m*)
winter	l'hiver (*m*)
in spring	au printemps
in summer/autumn/winter	en été/automne/hiver
during the summer	pendant l'été

The time

What's the time?	**L'heure (f)**
What time is it?	Quelle heure est-il?
It's seven o'clock	Il est sept heures
It's five past two	Il est deux heures cinq
It's a quarter past nine	Il est neuf heures et quart
It's half past four	Il est quatre heures et demie
It's twenty to six	Il est six heures moins vingt
It's a quarter to one	Il est une heure moins le quart
It's twelve o'clock/noon/ midnight	Il est midi/minuit
It's half past twelve	Il est midi et demi (noon)
	Il est minuit et demi (midnight)
At 16.25	A seize heures vingt-cinq
At 14.45	A quatorze heures quarante-cinq
At 18.00	A dix-huit heures
a.m.	du matin
p.m. (until 5 p.m.)	de l'après-midi
p.m. (after 5 p.m.)	du soir
at five o'clock in the morning	à cinq heures du matin

Weather — Le temps

What's the weather like?	Quel temps fait-il?
It's hot/cold/cool	Il fait chaud/froid/frais
It's sunny/windy	Il fait du soleil/du vent
It's raining/snowing	Il pleut/neige
It's freezing	Il gèle
It's foggy	Il fait du brouillard
The weather is fine/bad	Il fait beau/mauvais (temps)

à bientôt	see you soon
à bord	on board (ship)
à cause de	because of
à côté de	beside
à demain	see you tomorrow
l'abeille (*f*)	bee
abîmer	to spoil
l'abonné (*m*)	subscriber
d'abord	first of all
aboyer	to bark
l'abri (*m*)	shelter
l'abricot (*m*)	apricot
absent	absent
absolument	absolutely
accélérer	to accelerate
l'accent (*m*)	accent
accepter	to accept
l'accident (*m*)	accident
accompagner	to accompany
D'accord!	Okay!
l'accueil (*m*)	welcome
accueillir	to welcome
l'achat (*m*)	purchase
acheter	to buy
l'acteur (*m*)/l'actrice (*f*)	actor/actress
actif (*m*)/active (*f*)	active
les actualités (*f*)	news (e.g. on TV)
actuellement	at present
l'addition (*f*)	bill (e.g. in a café)
admirer	to admire
adorer	to adore

l'adresse (*f*)	address
s'adresser	to apply to
l'adulte (*m or f*)	adult
l'aéroglisseur (*m*)	hovercraft
l'aéroport (*m*)	airport
les affaires (*f*)	business
l'affiche (*f*)	poster
affreux (*m*)/affreuse (*f*)	frightful
l'agence de voyages (*f*)	travel agency
l'agent de police (*m*)	policeman
s'agir de	to concern
l'agneau (*m*)	lamb
agréable	pleasant
agréer	to accept
aider	to help
aigu (*m*)/aiguë (*f*)	sharp
l'ail (*m*)	garlic
ailleurs	elsewhere
aimable	likeable
aimer	to like; to love
aîné	older
en plein air	in the open air
l'alimentation (*f*)	grocery
allemand/l'Allemagne (*f*)	German/Germany
aller	to go
l'aller simple (*m*)	single ticket
l'aller-retour (*m*)	return ticket
allumer	to light
l'allumette (*f*)	match (e.g. for fire)
alors	then
l'alpinisme (*m*)	mountaineering
l'ambiance (*f*)	atmosphere

améliorer	to improve
l'amende (*f*)	fine (i.e. money)
amener	to bring
américain/l'Amérique (*f*)	American/America
l'ami (*m*)/**l'amie** (*f*)	friend
l'amitié (*f*)	friendship
l'amour (*m*)	love
l'ampoule (*f*)	bulb (electric)
amusant	amusing
s'amuser	to have a good time
l'an (*m*)/**l'année** (*f*)	year
l'ananas (*m*)	pineapple
anglais/l'Angleterre (*f*)	English/England
l'annonce (*f*)	advertisement
l'annuaire (*m*)	telephone directory
antiseptique	antiseptic
l'appareil-photo (*m*)	camera
l'appartement (*m*)	flat (i.e. an apartment)
apporter	to bring
apprendre	to learn
appuyer	to press
après-demain	the day after tomorrow
l'arbitre (*m*)	referee
l'arbre (*m*)	tree
l'argent (*m*)	money
l'armoire (*f*)	wardrobe
l'arrêt d'autobus (*m*)	bus-stop
s'arrêter	to stop
arroser	to water
l'ascenseur (*m*)	lift

l'**aspirateur** (*m*)	vacuum-cleaner
l'**aspirine** (*f*)	aspirin
s'**asseoir**	to sit down
assez	enough
l'**assiette** (*f*)	plate
assister à	to be present at
l'**atelier** (*m*)	workshop; studio
attendre	to wait for
atterrir	to land (e.g. a plane)
attraper	to catch
l'**auberge** de jeunesse (*f*)	youth hostel
aucun	*by* no *means, any*
augmenter	to increase
aujourd'hui	today
aussi	also
autant	as much
l'**autobus** (*m*)	bus
l'**autocar** (*m*)	coach (vehicle)
l'**autoroute** (*f*)	motorway
l'**autostop** (*m*)	hitch-hiking
autour de	around
autrefois	in the past
autrement	otherwise
avaler	to swallow
avant-hier	the day before yesterday
avec	with
l'**avenir** (*m*)	future
l'**averse** (*f*)	shower (of rain)
l'**avion** (*m*)	aeroplane
à mon **avis**	in my opinion
l'**avocat** (*m*)	lawyer

avoir l'air	to seem
avoir besoin de	to need
avoir chaud	to be hot
avoir envie de	to want to
avoir faim	to be hungry
avoir froid	to be cold
avoir honte	to be ashamed
avoir lieu	to take place
avoir mal à la tête	to have a headache
en **avoir** marre	to be fed up
avoir peur	to be frightened
avoir raison	to be right
avoir soif	to be thirsty
avoir sommeil	to be sleepy
avoir tort	to be wrong
avouer	to admit

_____   _____
_____   _____
_____   _____
_____   _____
_____   _____

le **bac**	sink (for washing)
le **bac**(calauréat)	exam (pre-university)
les **bagages** (*m*)	luggage
la **bague**	ring (e.g. on a finger)
la **baguette**	loaf
se **baigner**	to bathe
la **baignoire**	bath (tub)
le **bain**	bath
le **bal**	dance (that you go to)
balayer	to sweep
le **ballon**	ball
la **banane**	banana
le **banc**	bench
la **bande** dessinée	cartoon
la **banlieue**	suburb
la **banque**	bank (e.g. in the High Street)
la **barrière**	gate
en **bas**	downstairs
là- **bas**	over there; down there
le **bateau**	boat
le **bâtiment**	building
bâtir	to build
se **battre**	to fight
bavarder	to chatter
beau (*m*)/**belle** (*f*)	beautiful
beaucoup	a lot

le **beau-père**	father-in-law
le **bébé**	baby
belge/la **Belgique**	Belgian/Belgium
la **belle-mère**	mother-in-law
le **besoin**	need
la **bête**	animal
le **beurre**	butter
la **bibliothèque**	library
la **bicyclette**	bicycle
bien sûr	of course
bientôt	soon
bienvenu	welcome
Bienvenue!	Welcome!
la **bière**	beer
le **bifteck**	steak
le **bijou**	jewel
le **billet**	ticket
le **billet** de banque	banknote
la **biologie**	biology
la **bise**	kiss
le **bistro**	bar (selling drinks)
bizarre	strange
la **blague**	joke
blanc (*m*)/**blanche** (*f*)	white
blessé	injured
bleu	blue
le **bloc sanitaire**	toilet-block
le **boeuf**	bullock; beef
boire	to drink
le **bois**	wood
la **boisson**	drink

la **boîte**	box
la **boîte** aux lettres	letter-box
le **bol**	bowl
bon marché	cheap
le **bonbon**	sweet
Bonne Année!	Happy New Year!
de **bonne heure**	early
au **bord de**	at the edge of
la **bouche**	mouth
le **boucher**	butcher
la **boucherie**	butcher's shop
bouger	to move
le **boulanger**	baker
la **boulangerie**	bakery
les **boules** (*f*)	bowls
le **boulevard**	avenue
bouleverser	to upset
la **boum**	party (a get-together)
au **bout de**	at the end of
la **bouteille**	bottle
la **boutique**	shop
le **bouton**	button
le **bras**	arm (of the body)
bref (*m*)/**brève** (*f*)	brief
le **bricolage**	do-it-yourself
le **briquet**	lighter (cigarettes)
britannique	British
se **bronzer**	to suntan
la **brosse**	brush
se **brosser**	to brush yourself

le **brouillard**	fog
le **bruit**	noise
brûler	to burn
la **brume**	mist
brun	brown
bruyant	noisy
le **buffet**	sideboard
le **buisson**	bush
le **bureau de change**	exchange office
le **bureau des objets trouvés**	lost-property office
le **bureau de poste**	post office
le **bureau de renseignements**	information office
le **but**	goal

_____ _____
_____ _____
_____ _____
_____ _____
_____ _____

AB**C**DEFGHIJKLMNOPQRSTUVWXYZ

la **cabine** téléphonique	telephone box
cacher	to hide
le **cadeau**	present (that you give)
cadet (*m*)/**cadette** (*f*)	younger
le **café** au lait	coffee with milk (large)

le **café** crème	coffee with milk (small)
la **cafetière**	coffee-pot
le **cahier**	exercise book
la **caisse**	cash desk
calme	calm
le/la **camarade**	friend
le **cambrioleur**	burglar
le **camion**	lorry
la **camionnette**	van
la **campagne**	countryside
camper	to camp
le **campeur**	camper
faire du **camping**	to go camping
le **Canada**	Canada
canadien (*m*)/ **canadienne** (*f*)	Canadian
le **canapé**	sofa
le **canard**	duck (the bird)
le **canif**	penknife
la **canne** à pêche	fishing-rod
car	for (because)
la **caravane**	caravan
le **carnet** de chèques	cheque-book
la **carotte**	carrot
carré	square (shape)
le **carrefour**	crossroads
la **carrière**	career
la **carte**	card; map
la **carte** bancaire	banker's card
la **carte** de crédit	credit card

la **carte** postale	a postcard
la **carte** routière	map (of roads)
dans ce **cas**	in that case
casser	to break
la **casserole**	saucepan
la **cathédrale**	cathedral
à **cause** de	because of
causer	to chat
la **cave**	cellar
ce/cet/cette	this
la **ceinture** de sécurité	seat-belt
célèbre	famous
célibataire	single (not married)
le **cendrier**	an ashtray
le **centre**	centre
cependant	however
la **cerise**	cherry
certainement	certainly
cesser de	to stop (doing something)
c'est-à-dire	that is to say
chacun (*m*)/**chacune** (*f*)	each one
la **chaîne**	channel (on TV)
la **chaise**	chair
la **chaleur**	heat
la **chambre**	bedroom
le **champ**	field
le **champignon**	mushroom
le **championnat**	championship
la **chance**	luck
le **chandail**	sweater

changer	to change
le changement	change
la chanson	song
chanter	to sing
le chanteur/la chanteuse	singer
le chapeau	hat
le charbon	coal
chaque	each
la charcuterie	pork-butcher's
le chariot	trolley (super-market)
charmant	charming
la chasse	hunting
le chat	cat
le château	castle
chaud	hot
le chauffage central	central heating
le chauffeur	driver
la chaussée	roadway
la chaussette	sock
la chaussure	shoe
le chef	chief
le chemin de fer	railway
la chemise	shirt
le chemisier	blouse
le chèque de voyage	traveller's cheque
cher (*m*)/chère (*f*)	dear
chercher	to look for
le cheval	horse
les cheveux (*m*)	hair
chez	at the home of

le **chien**	dog
la **chimie**	chemistry
le **chocolat**	chocolate
choisir	to choose
le **choix**	choice
le **chômage**	unemployment
la **chose**	thing
le **chou**	cabbage
chouette	nice
le **chou-fleur**	cauliflower
le **cidre**	cider
le **ciel**	sky
le **cinéma**	cinema
la **circulation**	traffic
les **ciseaux** (*m*)	scissors
le **citron**	lemon
clair	clear
la **clé**/la **clef**	key
le **client**	customer
le **climat**	climate
la **cloche**	bell
le **cochon**	pig
le **code de la route**	the highway code
le **cœur**	heart
le **coiffeur**	hairdresser
le **coin**	corner
le **colis**	parcel
les **collants** (*m*)	tights
collectionner	to collect
coller	to stick
la **colline**	hill

la **collision**	collision
combien	how much; how many
commander	to order (e.g. a meal)
comme	like
commencer	to begin
comment	how
le **commerçant**	tradesman
le **commissariat**	police station
faire des **commissions**	to run errands
le **compartiment**	compartment (in a train)
complet (*m*)/**complète** (*f*)	full (bus, hotel)
composer	to dial
composter	to stamp (a ticket)
comprendre	to understand
le **comprimé**	tablet
compris	included
le **comptable**	accountant
compter	to count
le **concert**	concert
le/la **concierge**	caretaker
le **concombre**	cucumber
le **concours**	competition
le **conducteur**	driver
conduire	to drive (a vehicle) to lead
la **confiture**	jam
le **confort**	comfort
confortable	comfortable

en congé	on holiday
le congélateur	freezer
faire la connaissance de	to make the acquaintance of
connaître	to know (a person or a place)
conseiller	to advise
la consigne	left-luggage office
construire	to build
content	happy
continuer	to continue
au contraire	on the contrary
contre	against
contrôler	to check (tickets)
le copain/la copine	friend
le corps	body
la correspondance	connection (e.g. trains)
le/la correspondant(e)	pen friend
corriger	to correct
le costume	suit
la côte	coast
à côté de	beside
la côtelette	chop (e.g. pork)
la cotisation	subscription (to a club)
le coton hydrophile	cotton wool
le cou	neck
se coucher	to go to bed
coudre	to sew
la couleur	colour

le **couloir**	corridor
le **coup** de main	helping hand
le **coup** de soleil	sunstroke
le **coup** de téléphone	telephone call
✓ tout à **coup**	suddenly
couper	to cut
la **cour**	playground
courir	to run
le **courrier**	the mail
faire les **courses**	to do the shopping
le **cousin**/la **cousine**	cousin
le **coussin**	cushion
le **couteau**	knife
coûter	to cost
mettre le	
couvert	to lay the table
la **couverture**	blanket
couvrir	to cover
le **crabe**	crab
la **cravate**	tie (that you wear)
le **crayon**	pencil
la **crémerie**	dairy
la **crêpe**	pancake
crevé	punctured
crier	to shout
la **crise** de nerfs	attack of nerves
croire	to believe
la **cuiller**/**cuillère**	spoon
le **cuir**	leather
cuire	to cook
la **cuisine**	kitchen
la **cuisinière**	cooker

cultiver	to grow (e.g. plants)
le curé	priest
le/la cycliste	cyclist

_____   _____
_____   _____
_____   _____
_____   _____
_____   _____

d'abord	first of all
le/la dactylographe	typist
la dame	lady
dangereux (m)/-euse (f)	dangerous
danser	to dance
la date	date
debout	standing
le début	beginning
déchirer	to tear
décider	to decide
découvrir	to discover
décrire	to describe
décrocher	to lift (phone receiver)
déçu	disappointed
dedans	inside
là- dedans	inside
Défense de …	Do not … (It is forbidden to …)

dégoûtant	disgusting
dehors	outside
déjà	already
déjeuner	to have lunch
demain	tomorrow
demander	to ask (inquire)
démarrer	to start (e.g. a car)
déménager	to move house
demeurer	to live (reside)
demi	half
la dent	tooth
le dentifrice	toothpaste
le/la dentiste	dentist
dépanner	to repair (a car)
le départ	departure
le département	county
se dépêcher	to hurry
ça dépend	it depends
dépenser	to spend
depuis	since (with time)
déranger	to disturb
dernier (*m*)/dernière (*f*)	last
derrière	behind
désagréable	unpleasant
descendre	to go down
se déshabiller	to undress
désirer	to want
désolé	very sorry
le dessert	dessert
le dessin	drawing
dessous	below
dessus	above

détester	to hate
deuxième	second (i.e. after first)
devant	in front of
devenir	to become
la **déviation**	detour (that you make)
devoir	to have to
les **devoirs** (*m*)	homework
la **diarrhée**	diarrhoea
Dieu (*m*)	God
difficile	difficult
dîner	to have dinner
dire	to say, to tell
le **directeur**/la **directrice**	headmaster/mistress
se **diriger** vers	to head for
la **disco**	disco
discuter	to discuss
disparaître	to disappear
le **disque**	record (that you play)
divorcé	divorced
une **dizaine**	ten (approx.)
le **docteur**	doctor
le **doigt**	finger
le **domicile**	residence
Quel **dommage!**	What a pity!
donc	so (therefore)
donner	to give
dont	whose (not in questions)

dormir	to sleep
le **dortoir**	dormitory
le **dos**	back (part of body)
la **douane**	customs
le **douanier**	customs officer
doubler	to overtake
doucement	gently
la **douche**	shower (e.g. in bathroom)
la **douleur**	pain
sans **doute**	without doubt
doux (*m*)/**douce** (*f*)	sweet
une **douzaine**	dozen
le **drap**	sheet
le **drapeau**	flag
tout **droit**	straight on
à **droite**	on the right
drôle	funny
dur	hard
la **durée**	duration
durer	to last

QUAND
Lorsque

Amener
Apporter

NOTE:
Your new television includes a special circuit which protects your TV set in the event of a momentary power surge. On the infrequent occasions when this circuit is called upon to provide this protection, the TV set will shut itself off. If such an event should ever occur, first unplug the TV from the electrical outlet, then replug the power cord and turn the TV set back on.

EL 4311-1

l'eau (*f*)	water
l'échange (*f*)	exchange
échanger	to exchange
l'écharpe (*f*)	scarf (lady's)
les échecs (*m*)	chess
l'échelle (*f*)	ladder
échouer	to fail
l'école (*f*)	school
économiser	to save (money)
écossais/l'Écosse (*f*)	Scottish/Scotland
écouter	to listen
l'écran (*m*)	screen
écraser	to crush
écrire	to write
en effet	in fact
égal	equal
l'église (*f*)	church
l'électricien (*m*)	electrician
l'électricité (*f*)	electricity
élégant	smart (i.e. well-dressed)
l'élève (*m or f*)	pupil
s'éloigner	to go away
embarquer	to board (a ship)
l'embouteillage (*m*)	traffic jam
embrasser	to kiss
l'embrayage (*m*)	clutch (on a car)
l'émission	broadcast
emmener	to take (a person)
empêcher	to prevent
l'emplacement (*m*)	pitch (e.g. on camp site)

l'emploi (*m*)	job
l'emploi (*m*) du temps	timetable (in a school)
l'employé (*m*)/ l'employée (*f*)	employee
employer	to use
emporter	to take away
emprunter	to borrow
enchanté	pleased to meet you
encore	again
s'endormir	to fall asleep
l'endroit (*m*)	place
énervé	annoyed
l'enfant (*m or f*)	child
enfin	finally
enlever	to remove
s'ennuyer	to be bored
ennuyeux (*m*)/ennuyeuse (*f*)	boring
énorme	enormous
enrhumé	having a cold
l'enseignement (*m*)	education
enseigner	to teach
ensemble	together
ensoleillé	sunny
ensuite	then
entendre	to hear
bien entendu	of course
entier (*m*)/entière (*f*)	entire
entouré de	surrounded by
entre	between

l'entrée (f)	entrance
entrer	to enter
l'entrevue (f)	interview
l'enveloppe (f)	envelope
l'envie (f)	desire
environ	about
envoyer	to send
épais (m)/épaisse (f)	thick
l'épaule (f)	shoulder
épeler	to spell
l'épicerie (f)	grocer's
l'épicier (m)	grocer
les épinards (m)	spinach
éplucher	to peel
l'éponge (f)	sponge
l'époque (f)	period (of time)
l'épouse (f)	wife
épouser	to marry
l'épouvante (f)	fright
l'époux (m)	husband
l'équipe (f)	team
l'équitation (f)	horse-riding
l'erreur (f)	mistake
l'escalier (m)	stairs
l'escalier roulant (m)	escalator
l'escargot (m)	snail
espagnol/l'Espagne (f)	Spanish/Spain
l'espèce (f)	type
espérer	to hope
l'espoir (m)	hope
essayer	to try

l'essence (f)	petrol
essentiel (m)/-ielle (f)	essential
essoufflé	out of breath
l'essuie-mains (m)	towel
essuyer	to wipe
l'estomac (m)	stomach
l'étage (m)	floor (storey)
l'étagère (f)	shelf
les Etats-Unis (m)	the United States
l'été (m)	summer
éteindre	to put out (a light)
l'étoile (m)	star (in the sky)
étonnant	astonishing
étonner	to astonish
l'étranger (m)/ l'étrangère (f)	foreigner
à l'étranger	abroad
étroit	narrow
les études (f)	studies
l'étudiant (m)/l'étudiante (f)	student
étudier	to study
européen (m)/ européenne (f)	European
eux	them
s'évanouir	to faint
l'événement (m)	event
évidemment	evidently
l'évier (m)	sink (for washing)
l'évier à deux bacs	double sink unit
exact	correct
exagérer	to exaggerate

l'examen (*m*)	exam
s'excuser	to apologize
par exemple	for example
exprès	on purpose
expliquer	to explain
extrêmement	extremely

_____ _____
_____ _____
_____ _____
_____ _____
_____ _____

en **face** de	opposite
fâché	angry
facile	easy
le **facteur**	postman
la **facture**	invoice
faible	weak
avoir **faim**	to be hungry
faire	to do
faire attention	to be careful
tout à **fait**	completely
la **falaise**	cliff
falloir	to be necessary
la **famille**	family
la **farine**	flour

fatigué	tired
le **faubourg**	suburb
il **faut**	it is necessary
la **faute**	lack; fault
le **fauteuil**	armchair
faux (*m*)/**fausse** (*f*)	false
favori (*m*)/**-ite** (*f*)	favourite
félicitations (*f*)	congratulations
féliciter	to congratulate
la **femme**	wife; woman
la **fenêtre**	window
la **ferme**	farm
fermer	to close
le **ferry**	ferry
la **fête**	holiday
fêter	to celebrate (birthday, Christmas)
le **feu**	fire
le **feu rouge**	traffic light
les **fiançailles** (*f*)	engagement (to be wed)
la **fiche**	form (to fill in)
fier (*m*)/**fière** (*f*)	proud
la **fièvre**	high temperature (fever)
la **figure**	face
le **filet**	net
la **fille**	daughter
la jeune **fille**	girl
le **fils**	son
la **fin**	end

	finalement	finally
	finir	to finish
la	**fleur**	flower
le	**fleuve**	river (large)
le	**flic**	policeman (slang)
la	**foire**	fair
une	**fois**	once
	foncé	dark (colour)
le/la	**fonctionnaire**	civil servant
	fonctionner	to function
le	**fond**	the bottom (e.g. of a well)
le	**football**	football
la	**forêt**	forest
la	**forme**	shape
	formidable	marvellous
	fort	strong
	fou (*m*)/**folle** (*f*)	mad
la	**foule**	crowd
le	**four**	oven
la	**fourchette**	fork (cutlery)
	fournir	to supply
	fragile	fragile
	frais (*m*)/**fraîche** (*f*)	cool
la	**fraise**	strawberry
la	**framboise**	raspberry
	franc (*m*)/**franche** (*f*)	frank
	français/la **France**	French/France
	franchement	frankly
	frapper	to hit
le	**frein**	brake

freiner	to brake
le frère	brother
le frigo	fridge
les frites (*f*)	chips
froid	cold
le fromage	cheese
la frontière	frontier
le fruit	fruit
les fruits de mer (*m*)	seafood
la fuite d'eau	leak (water)
la fumée	smoke
fumer	to smoke
furieux (*m*)/-ieuse (*f*)	furious
le fusil	rifle

———————————   ———————————

———————————   ———————————

———————————   ———————————

———————————   ———————————

ABCDEF**G**HIJKLMNOPQRSTUVWXYZ

gagner	to earn (e.g. money)
gai	happy
gallois/le Pays de Galles	Welsh/Wales
le gant	glove
le garage	garage
le garagiste	mechanic
garantir	to guarantee

le garçon	waiter (in a café); boy
garder	to keep
le gardien	attendant (in a museum)
la gare	station
la gare routière	bus-station
garer	to park
le gâteau	cake
à gauche	to the left
le gaz	gas
geler	to freeze
le gendarme	policeman
gêner	to impede; to bother
en général	in general
généralement	generally
généreux (*m*)/ généreuse (*f*)	generous
le genou	knee
les gens (*m*)	people
gentil (*m*)/gentille (*f*)	nice
la géographie	geography
la glace	ice (-cream)
glisser	to slip
la gomme	rubber
gonflé	swollen
gonfler	to blow up (a tyre)
la gorge	throat
le gouvernement	government
le goût	taste
goûter	to taste

la **goutte**	drop (e.g. of water)
grâce à	thanks to
le **gramme**	gram(me)
la **Grande-Bretagne**	Great Britain
la **grand-mère**	grandmother
le **grand-père**	grandfather
gras (*m*)/**grasse** (*f*)	fat
gratuit	free (no charge)
grave	serious
grec (*m*)/**grecque** (*f*)	Greek
la **Grèce**	Greece
la **grêle**	hail
le **grenier**	attic
la **grenouille**	frog
la **grève**	strike (i.e. stopping work)
grimper	to climb
la **grippe**	influenza
gris	grey
gros (*m*)/**grosse** (*f*)	big
le **groupe**	group
guérir	to cure
la **guerre**	war
le **guichet**	ticket office
le **guide**	guide
la **guitare**	guitar
la **gymnastique**	gymnastics

habile	clever
s'**habiller**	to dress yourself
l'**habitant** (*m*)	inhabitant
habiter	to live (reside)
d'**habitude**	usually
les **haricots** (*m*)	beans
à la **hâte**	in haste
en **haut**	upstairs
là-**haut**	up there
l'**hebdomadaire** (*m*)	magazine (weekly)
héberger	to put someone up
Hélas!	Alas!
l'**herbe** (*f*)	grass
hésiter	to hesitate
à l'**heure**	on time
À quelle **heure?**	At what time?
À tout à l'**heure!**	See you soon!
de bonne **heure**	early
heureusement	fortunately
heureux (*m*)/**heureuse** (*f*)	happy
se **heurter**	to knock against
hier	yesterday
l'**histoire** (*f*)	history
l'**hiver** (*m*)	winter
le **hockey**	hockey
hollandais/la **Hollande**	Dutch/the Netherlands
l'**homme** (*m*)	man
honnête	honest

avoir **honte**	to be ashamed
l'**hôpital** (*m*)	hospital
l'**horaire** (*m*)	timetable (at a station)
l'**horloge** (*f*)	clock
l'**hors d'oeuvre** (*m*)	starter (in a restaurant)
l'**hospitalité** (*f*)	hospitality
l'**hôtel** (*m*)	hotel
l'**hôtel** de ville (*m*)	town hall
l'**hôtesse** de l'air (*f*)	air hostess
l'**huile** (*f*)	oil
l'**huître** (*f*)	oyster
humide	damp
l'**hypermarché** (**m**)	hypermarket

_____   _____
_____   _____
_____   _____
_____   _____

ABCDEFGH**I**JKLMNOPQRSTUVWXYZ

ici	here
l'**idée** (*f*)	idea
ignorer	to be ignorant of
il y a	there is; there are
l'**île** (*f*)	an island
l'**image** (*f*)	a picture (e.g. in a book)

immédiatement	immediately
immense	immense
l'**immeuble** (*m*)	block of flats
immobile	motionless
l'**imperméable** (*m*)	raincoat
impoli	rude
important	important
n'**importe**	it doesn't matter
impossible	impossible
l'**impôt** (*m*)	tax
l'**impression** (*f*)	an impression
impressionnant	impressive
l'**incendie** (*m*)	fire (e.g. in a building)
inconnu	unknown
incroyable	incredible
l'**indigestion** (*f*)	indigestion
indiquer	to point to
l'**industrie** (*f*)	industry
industriel (*m*)/**-ielle** (*f*)	industrial
l'**infirmière** (*f*)	nurse
l'**information** (*f*)	information
les **informations** (*f*)	news (e.g. on TV)
informer	to inform
l'**ingénieur** (*m*)	engineer
inquiet (*m*)/**inquiète** (*f*)	worried
s'**inquiéter**	to worry
l'**insecte** (*m*)	insect
l'**insolation** (*f*)	sunstroke
s'**installer**	to settle (e.g. in a chair)

l'instant (*m*)	instant
l'instituteur (*m*)/-trice (*f*)	teacher (primary)
l'instrument (*m*)	instrument
insulter	to insult
insupportable	unbearable
intelligent	intelligent
l'intention (*f*)	intention
interdire	to forbid
Interdit de ...	It is forbidden to ...
intéressant	interesting
s'intéresser à	to be interested in
l'intérêt (*m*)	interest
introduire	to insert (e.g. a coin)
inutile	useless
l'invitation (*f*)	invitation
inviter	to invite
irlandais/l'Irlande (*f*)	Irish/Ireland
Italie (*f*)	Italy
italien (*m*)/-ienne (*f*)	Italian

jaloux (*m*)/**jalouse** (*f*)	jealous
ne … **jamais**	never
la **jambe**	leg
le **jambon**	ham
le **jardin**	garden
le **jardinage**	gardening
jaune	yellow
le **jean**	jeans
jeter	to throw
le **jeton**	token (for using phone)
le **jeu**	game
jeune	young
la **jeunesse**	youth
joli	pretty
jouer	to play
le **jouet**	toy
le **joueur**	player
le **jour** férié	public holiday
le **journal**	newspaper
la **journée**	day
juger	to judge
le **jumeau**/la **jumelle**	twin
le **jumelage**	twinning (of towns)
la **jupe**	skirt
jurer	to swear
le **jus** de fruit	fruit juice
jusqu'à	until
juste	correct

le **kilo**	kilogram(me)
le **kilomètre**	kilometre
le **kiosque**	kiosk
klaxonner	to sound the horn

_____   _____
_____   _____
_____   _____
_____   _____
_____   _____
_____

ABCDEFGHIJK**L**MNOPQRSTUVWXYZ

là	there
là-bas	over there; down there
là-dedans	inside
là-haut	up there
le **laboratoire**	laboratory
le **lac**	lake
laid	ugly
la **laine**	wool
laisser	to let
laisser tomber	to drop
le **lait**	milk
la **laitue**	lettuce
la **lampe**	lamp
lancer	to throw
la **langue**	tongue; language
le **lapin**	rabbit

large	wide
le **lavabo**	a washbasin
se **laver**	to wash yourself
le **lave-vaisselle**	dishwasher
la **laverie** automatique	launderette
la **leçon**	lesson
la **lecture**	reading
léger (*m*)/**légère** (*f*)	light (i.e. not heavy)
le **légume**	vegetable
le **lendemain**	(the) next day
lent	slow
lentement	slowly
faire la **lessive**	to do the washing
la **lettre**	letter
leur	their
la **levée**	collection (of mail)
se **lever**	to get up
la **lèvre**	lip
la **liberté**	liberty
la **librairie**	bookshop
libre	free
le **lieu**	place
au **lieu** de	instead of
la **ligne**	line
la **limonade**	lemonade
lire	to read
la **liste**	list
le **lit**	bed
le **litre**	litre
le **livre**	book
la **livre**	pound (weight)

la **livre** sterling	pound (money)
la **location**	hiring
loger	to lodge
la **loi**	law
loin	far
les **loisirs** (m)	spare time
le **long** de	along
longtemps	a long time
lorsque	when
louer	to hire
lourd	heavy
le **loyer**	rent
la **lumière**	light
la **lune**	moon
les **lunettes** (f)	glasses (spectacles)
lutter	to struggle
le **luxe**	luxury
le **lycée**	school (secondary)

_____   _____

ABCDEFGHIJKL**M**NOPQRSTUVWXYZ

la **machine** à coudre	sewing-machine
la **machine** à écrire	typewriter
la **machine** à laver	washing-machine

le **magasin**	shop
le **magazine**	magazine
le **magnétophone**	tape recorder
le **magnétoscope**	video recorder
magnifique	magnificent
maigre	thin
le **maillot de bain**	bathing costume
la **main**	hand
maintenant	now
le **maire**	mayor
la **mairie**	town hall
mais	but
la **maison**	house
la **maison des jeunes**	youth club
le **maître**	master
la **maîtresse**	mistress
la **majuscule**	capital letter
le **mal aux dents**	toothache
le **mal de mer**	seasickness
le **mal de tête**	headache
le **mal au ventre**	stomach-ache
malade	sick
la **maladie**	an illness
malgré	despite
malheureusement	unfortunately
malheureux (*m*)/**-euse** (*f*)	unhappy
la **Manche**	the English Channel
manger	to eat
la **manière**	manner
la **manifestation**	demonstration

manquer	to miss (e.g. the train)
le manteau	coat
le maquillage	make-up
le marchand de fruits	fruit-seller
le marchand de légumes	greengrocer
le marché	market
bon marché	cheap
marcher	to walk
le mari	husband
se marier avec	to marry
la marque	make (e.g. of car)
marron	brown (chestnut)
le match	match (e.g. football)
le matelas	mattress
les mathématiques (f)	maths
la matière	subject (at school)
le matin	morning
mauvais	bad
le mécanicien	mechanic
méchant	nasty; spiteful
le médecin	doctor
le médicament	medicine
meilleur	better; best (adj)
le membre	member
même	even
la même chose	the same thing
tout de même	all the same
menacer	to threaten
faire le ménage	to do the housework
mener	to lead

mentir	to lie (tell untruths)
le **menton**	chin
le **menu**	menu
la **mer**	sea
le **mal** de	
mer	seasickness
merci	thank you
la **mère**	mother
merveilleux (*m*)/**-euse** (*f*)	marvellous
le **message**	message
le **métal**	metal
la **météo**	weather forecast
le **métier**	job
le **mètre**	metre
le **métro**	the underground (trains)
mettre	to put
mettre à la poste	to post (a letter)
se **mettre** en colère	to get angry
se **mettre** en route	to set off
meublé	furnished
les **meubles** (*m*)	furniture
le **micro-ordinateur**	microcomputer
midi	midday
le **Midi**	the South of France
le **miel**	honey
mieux	better; best (*adv*)
mignon (*m*)/**mignonne** (*f*)	adorable
au **milieu** de	in the middle of
mille (*m*)	(a) thousand
le **million**	million

	mince	slim
	minuit (*m*)	midnight
la	**minute**	minute
le	**miroir**	mirror
	mi-temps	half-time (in sport)
la	**mode**	fashion
	moderne	modern
	moins	less
la	**moitié**	half
le	**moment**	moment
tout le	**monde**	everybody
la	**monnaie**	change (i.e. small change)
la	**montagne**	mountain
	monter	to go up
	montrer	to show
le	**monument**	monument
le	**morceau**	piece
	mordre	to bite
	mort	dead
le	**mot**	word
le	**moteur**	engine
la	**moto**	motorbike
la	**mouche**	fly
le	**mouchoir**	handkerchief
	mouillé	wet
les	**moules** (*f*)	mussels
	mourir	to die
la	**moutarde**	mustard
le	**mouton**	sheep
le	**mouvement**	movement

le **mur**	wall
le **musée**	museum
le **musicien**	musician
la **musique**	music

_____ _____
_____ _____
_____ _____
_____ _____
_____ _____

ABCDEFGHIJKLM**N**OPQRSTUVWXYZ

nager	to swim
la **naissance**	birth
naître	to be born
la **nappe**	tablecloth
la **natation**	swimming
naturel (*m*)/**naturelle** (*f*)	natural
naturellement	naturally
le **navire**	ship
ne ... jamais	never
ne ... ni ... ni	neither ... nor
ne ... pas	not
ne ... personne	nobody
ne ... plus	no longer
ne ... que	only
ne ... rien	nothing
né	born

néanmoins	nevertheless
nécessaire	necessary
la neige	snow
neiger	to snow
nerveux (*m*)/-euse (*f*)	nervous
le nettoyage à sec	dry-cleaning
nettoyer	to clean
neuf (*m*)/neuve (*f*)	new (newly manu-factured)
le neveu	nephew
le nez	nose
ni … ni …	neither … nor …
le nid	nest
la nièce	niece
nier	to deny
le niveau	level
Noël (*m*)	Christmas
noir	black
le nom	name
le nombre	number (amount)
nombreux (*m*)/-euse (*f*)	numerous
non compris	not included
non plus	neither
le nord	the north
normalement	normally
la note	mark (in an exam)
notre (*s*)/nos (*pl*)	our
nourrir	to feed
la nourriture	food
nouveau (*m*)/-elle (*f*)	new
de nouveau	again

la **nouvelle**	news (an item of)
les **nouvelles** (*f*)	news
se **noyer**	to drown
nu	bare
le **nuage**	a cloud
nuageux (*m*)/**-euse** (*f*)	cloudy
la **nuit**	night
le **numéro**	number (house, page)
le **nylon**	nylon

_____   _____
_____   _____
_____   _____
_____   _____

ABCDEFGHIJKLMN**O**PQRSTUVWXYZ

obéir	to obey
les **objets trouvés** (*m*)	lost property
obligatoire	compulsory
obliger	to oblige
l'**occasion** (*f*)	opportunity
occupé	busy
l'**océan** (*m*)	ocean
l'**odeur** (*f*)	smell
l'**oeil**	eye
l'**oeuf** (*m*)	egg
l'**offre** (*f*)	offer

offrir	to offer
Oh là là!	Good heavens!
l'oie (*f*)	goose
l'oignon (*m*)	onion
l'oiseau (*m*)	bird
l'ombre (*f*)	shadow
l'omelette (*f*)	omelette
l'oncle (*m*)	uncle
l'ongle (*m*)	nail (e.g. a toe nail)
l'opéra (*m*)	opera
l'opération (*f*)	operation
l'opinion (*f*)	opinion
l'opticien (*m*)	optician
l'or (*m*)	gold
l'orage (*m*)	storm
orageux (*m*)/**-euse** (*f*)	stormy
l'orange (*f*)	orange
l'orchestre (*m*)	orchestra
ordinaire	ordinary
l'ordinateur (*m*)	computer
l'ordonnance (*f*)	prescription
l'ordre (*m*)	order
organiser	to organize
l'oreille (*f*)	ear
l'oreiller (*m*)	pillow
l'orteil (*m*)	toe
l'os (*m*)	bone
oser	to dare
ôter	to remove
ou	or
où	where

l'**ouate** hydrophile (f)	cotton wool
oublier	to forget
l'**ouest** (m)	the west
oui	yes
l'**ours** (m)	bear
l'**outil** (m)	tool
ouvert	open
l'**ouvre-boîtes** (m)	tin-opener
l'**ouvreuse** (f)	usherette
l'**ouvrier** (m)	
l'**ouvrière** (f)	worker
ouvrir	to open

ABCDEFGHIJKLMNO**P**QRSTUVWXYZ

la **page**	page (of book)
le **paiement**	payment
le **pain**	bread
la **paire**	pair
le **palais**	palace
pâle	pale
le **palier**	landing (upstairs)
le **panier**	basket
la **panne**	breakdown
en **panne**	broken down (of car)

le **pansement**	dressing (e.g. on a wound)
panser	to bandage
le **pantalon**	trousers
la **pantoufle**	slipper
le **papier**	paper
le **papier à lettres**	writing paper
le **papillon**	a butterfly
Pâques (*f*)	Easter
le **paquet**	parcel
par	through
par exemple	for example
par ici	this way
par jour	per day
paraître	to seem
le **parapluie**	umbrella
le **parc**	park
parce que	because
le **pardessus**	overcoat
pardon!	excuse me!
pardonner	to forgive
le **pare-brise**	windscreen
pareil (*m*)/**-eille** (*f*)	similar
les **parents** (*m*)	parents
paresseux (*m*)/**-euse** (*f*)	lazy
parfait	perfect
parfaitement	perfectly
le **parfum**	perfume
parisien (*m*)/**-ienne** (*f*)	Parisian
le **parking**	car park
parler	to speak; to talk

parmi	among
la **parole**	word
de la **part** de	on behalf of
partager	to share
participer	to take part in
en **particulier**	in particular
la **partie**	part (of a whole)
partir	to leave
à **partir** de	after
partout	everywhere
pas du tout	not at all
le **passage** à niveau	level crossing
le **passage** clouté	pedestrian crossing
le **passager**	passenger
le **passant**	passer-by
le **passeport**	passport
se **passer**	happen
le **passe-temps**	hobby
passionnant	exciting
la **pâte** dentifrice	toothpaste
patient	patient
patiner	to skate
la **pâtisserie**	cake shop
le **patron**	boss
pauvre	poor
payer	to pay
le **pays**	country
le **Pays** de Galles	Wales
le **paysage**	countryside
le **paysan**	peasant
le **péage**	toll

la **peau**	skin
la **pêche**	peach
faire la **pêche**	to go fishing
pêcher	to fish
le **peigne**	comb
se **peigner**	to comb your hair
à **peine**	scarcely
la **peinture**	painting
la **pelouse**	lawn
la **pellicule**	a film (for a camera)
pencher	to lean
pendant	during
pendant que	while
la **pendule**	clock
penser	to think
la **pension** complète	board and lodging
demi-**pension** (*f*)	half-board
perdre	to lose
se **perdre**	to get lost
le **père**	father
permanent	permanent
permettre	to allow
le **permis** de conduire	driving licence
la **personne**	person
ne ... **personne**	nobody
la **perte**	loss
le **petit** déjeuner	breakfast
le **petit-fils**	grandson
le **petit pois**	pea
la **petite-fille**	granddaughter
un **peu**	a little

à peu près	approximately
la **peur**	fear
peut-être	perhaps
le **phare**	headlight
la **pharmacie**	chemist's
le **pharmacien**	chemist
la **photo**	photo
le/la **photographe**	photographer
la **photographie**	photography; photograph
la **phrase**	sentence
le **piano**	piano
la **pièce**	room
la **pièce** d'identité	identification
la **pièce** de théâtre	play (e.g. at a theatre)
le **pied**	foot
la **pierre**	stone
le **piéton**	pedestrian
la **pile**	battery (small)
le **pilote**	pilot
la **pilule**	pill
le **ping-pong**	table tennis
le **pique-nique**	picnic
la **piqûre**	sting
pire	worse
la **piscine**	swimming-pool
pittoresque	picturesque
le **placard**	cupboard
la **place**	square (in a town)
le **plafond**	ceiling

la **plage**	beach
se **plaindre**	to complain
plaire	to please
la **plaisanterie**	joke
le **plaisir**	pleasure
s'il te (vous) **plaît**	Please
le **plan**	map (of town)
le **plancher**	the floor (of room)
la **plante**	plant
la **plaque** d'immatriculation	number plate
le **plat**	course (at dinner)
le **plateau**	tray
plein	full (container)
faire le **plein**	to fill up (with petrol)
pleurer	to cry
pleuvoir (à verse)	to rain (heavily)
le **plombier**	plumber
plonger	to dive
la **pluie**	rain
la **plupart**	most
plus	more
ne ... **plus**	no longer
plusieurs	several
plutôt	rather
pluvieux (*m*)/**-ieuse** (*f*)	rainy
le **pneu**	tyre
la **poche**	pocket
le **poêle**	stove
la **poêle**	frying-pan

le **poids**	weight
le **poids** lourd	lorry (large)
le **poignet**	the wrist
le **point**	point
à **point**	done to a turn (meat)
la **pointure**	size (shoes, etc)
la **poire**	pear
le **poireau**	leek
le **pois**	pea
le **poisson**	fish
la **poitrine**	chest (part of body)
le **poivre**	pepper
poli	polite
la **police**	the police
appeler **police** secours	to call the police
la **politesse**	politeness
la **pollution**	pollution
la **pomme**	apple
la **pomme** de terre	potato
le **pompier**	fireman
le/la **pompiste**	petrol-pump attendant
le **pont**	bridge
le **porc**	pig
le **port**	port
la **porte**	door
le **portefeuille**	wallet
le **porte-monnaie**	purse
porter	to carry
porter (des vêtements)	to wear (clothes)

le **porteur**	porter
la **portière**	door (of vehicle)
poser une question	to ask a question
poster	to post (a letter)
le **pot**	pot
potable	drinkable
le **potage**	soup
la **poubelle**	bin
la **poule**	hen
le **poulet**	chicken
pour	for
le **pourboire**	tip (e.g. to a waitress)
pour cent	per cent
pourquoi?	why?
pourtant	however
pousser	to push
la **poussière**	dust
pouvoir	to be able
pratique	useful
pratiquer	to practise
le **pré**	meadow
précieux (*m*)/-**ieuse** (*f*)	precious
préférer	to prefer
premier (*m*)/**première** (*f*)	first
le **Premier Ministre**	Prime Minister
prendre	to take
le **prénom**	first name
préparer	to prepare
près de	near
présent	present

présenter	to introduce (a person)
presque	almost
pressé	in a hurry
la **pression**	pressure
prêt	ready
prêter	to lend
prévoir	to foresee
je t'en (vous en) **prie**	don't mention it
prier	to ask (invite)
le **printemps**	spring (season)
priorité à droite	give way to traffic from right
la **prise** de courant	socket (electrical)
privé	private
le **prix**	price
probable	probable
le **problème**	problem
prochain	next
proche	near
le/la **professeur**	teacher (secondary)
la **profession**	profession
profiter	to take advantage of
profond	deep
le **programme**	programme (e.g. TV)
le **progrès**	progress
le **projet**	plan (e.g. for future)
la **promenade**	walk
la **promenade** à vélo	bike-ride
se **promener**	to go for a walk

promettre	to promise
prononcer	to pronounce
proposer	to suggest
propre	clean
le/la **propriétaire**	owner
protéger	to protect
protester	to protest
prouver	to prove
en **provenance** de	coming from (e.g. a train)
les **provisions** (*f*)	shopping
prudent	careful
la **prune**	plum
public (*m*)/**publique** (*f*)	public
la **publicité**	advertising
puis	then
puisque	since (because)
le **pull**(-over)	pullover
punir	to punish
pur	pure
le **pyjama**	pyjamas

_____   _____
_____   _____
_____   _____
_____   _____
_____   _____

le **quai**	platform (at station)
la **qualité**	quality
quand	when
quand même	all the same
la **quantité**	quantity
le **quart**	quarter
le **quartier**	district
quel (*m*)/**quelle** (*f*)?	which?
quelque chose	something
quelquefois	sometimes
quelque part	somewhere
quelqu'un	someone
la **question**	question
la **queue**	tail (of animal)
faire la **queue**	to queue
la **quinzaine**	fortnight
quitter	to leave
quotidien (*m*)/**-ienne** (*f*)	daily

_____   _____

_____   _____

_____   _____

_____   _____

ABCDEFGHIJKLMNOPQ**R**STUVWXYZ

raccommoder	to mend
raccrocher	to ring off (on phone)

raconter	to tell (e.g. a story)
le **radiateur**	radiator
la **radio**	radio
le **raisin**	grape
la **raison**	reason
avoir **raison**	to be right
ralentir	to slow down
ramasser	to gather
ramener	to bring back
ranger	to tidy (e.g. a room)
rapide	fast
rapidement	quickly
rappeler	to remind
se **rappeler**	to remember
rapporter	to bring back
rare	unusual
rarement	rarely
se **raser**	to shave
le **rasoir**	razor
rater	to fail (e.g. an exam)
ravi	delighted
le **rayon**	department (in a store)
en **réalité**	really
récemment	recently
récent	recent
le **récepteur**	receiver (phone; TV set)
la **réception**	the reception desk
la **recette**	recipe
recevoir	to receive

le **réchaud**	stove (e.g. for camping)
la **réclamation**	complaint
recommander	to recommend
recommencer	to start again
la **récompense**	reward
reconnaissant	grateful
reconnaître	to recognize
la **récréation**	break-time (at school)
le **reçu**	receipt
reculer	to move back
la **réduction**	reduction
réfléchir	to think
refuser	to refuse
regarder	to look
la **région**	region
la **règle**	rule; ruler (for measuring)
le **règlement**	regulation
regretter	to be sorry
regulier (*m*)/**-ière** (*f*)	regular
la **reine**	queen
remarquer	to notice
rembourser	to repay
le **remède**	remedy
remercier	to thank
se **remettre**	to recover (from illness)
remplir	to fill
remuer	to stir (coffee, etc)

le	**renard**	fox
	rencontrer	to meet
se	**rencontrer**	to meet (of two people or things)
le	**rendez-vous**	appointment (to meet)
	rendre	to give back
se	**rendre** compte	to realize
les	**renseignements** (*m*)	information
la	**rentrée**	return (to school)
	rentrer	to return (e.g. home)
	renverser	to knock over
	renvoyer	to sack (from job)
la	**réparation**	repair
	réparer	to repair
le	**repas**	meal
	repasser	to iron (clothes)
	répéter	to repeat
	répondre	to answer
se	**reposer**	to rest
la	**réservation**	reservation
	réserver	to reserve
	respirer	to breathe
	responsable	responsible
	ressembler	to look like
le	**restaurant**	restaurant
	rester	to stay
le	**résultat**	result
en	**retard**	late (behind schedule)
le	**retour**	return

retourner	to return
le rétroviseur	mirror (in a vehicle)
la réunion	meeting
réussir	to succeed
le réveil	alarm clock
se réveiller	to wake up
revenir	to return
rêver	to dream
au revoir	goodbye
la revue	magazine
le rez-de-chaussée	the ground floor
le rhume	cold (i.e. the illness)
riche	rich
le rideau	curtain
de rien	don't mention it
ne … rien	nothing
rire	to laugh
le risque	risk
la rive	bank (of river)
la rivière	river
le riz	rice
la robe	dress
le robinet	tap
le roi	king
le roman	novel
rond	round
le rond-point	roundabout (traffic)
la rose	rose
rôti	roast
la roue	wheel
la roue de secours	spare wheel

rouge	red
rouler	to drive along (travel)
la **route**	road (main)
roux (*m*)/**rousse** (*f*)	red (hair)
le **Royaume-Uni**	the United Kingdom
le **ruban**	ribbon
la **rue**	street
le **rugby**	rugby
le **ruisseau**	stream

_____   _____

_____   _____

_____   _____

_____   _____

ABCDEFGHIJKLMNOPQR**S**TUVWXYZ

le **sable**	sand
le **sac**	bag
le **sac à dos**	rucksack
le **sac à main**	handbag
le **sac de couchage**	sleeping bag
sage	well-behaved
saignant	rare (of steaks)
sain	healthy
la **saison**	season (of the year)
saisir	to seize
la **salade**	salad
le **salaire**	wage

sale	dirty
la salle à manger	dining-room
la salle d'attente	waiting-room
la salle de bains	bathroom
la salle de séjour	lounge
le salon	drawing-room
saluer	to greet
salut	hello
la sandale	sandal
le sandwich	sandwich
le sang	blood
sans	without
la santé	health
la sardine	sardine
satisfait	satisfied
la sauce	gravy
la saucisse	sausage (not pre-cooked)
le saucisson	sausage (pre-cooked)
sauf	except
le saumon	salmon
sauter	to jump
sauver	to save
se sauver	to run away
savoir	to know (a thing)
le savon	soap
la science	science
le scooter	scooter
la séance	performance (at cinema)
le seau	bucket

sec (*m*)/sèche (*f*)	dry
le sèche-cheveux	hair-dryer
le secours	help
le/la secrétaire	secretary
la section	section
le séjour	stay
le sel	salt
la semaine	week
sembler	to seem
sens interdit (*m*)	no entry
sens unique (*m*)	one-way system
le sentier	path
sentir	to feel
séparé	separated
sérieux (*m*)/-ieuse (*f*)	serious
le serpent	snake
serrer la main	to shake hands
le serveur	barman
la serveuse	barmaid
à votre service	at your service
service (non) compris	service (not) included
la serviette	towel
servir	to serve
se servir de	to use; to make use of
seul	alone
seulement	only
sévère	strict
le sexe	sex
le shampooing	shampoo

le **short**	(pair of) shorts
si	if
si (after a negative)	yes
si (with adjective)	so
le **siècle**	century
siffler	to whistle
la **signature**	signature
signer	to sign
le **silence**	silence
simple	simple
la **situation**	situation
situé	situated
le **slip**	underpants
social	social
la **société**	company (in business); society
la **sœur**	sister
la **soie**	silk
la **soif**	thirst
soigner	to look after
le **soin**	care (e.g. of children)
le **soir**	evening
la **soirée**	party (social gathering)
le **sol**	ground
le **soldat**	soldier
le **soleil**	sun
solide	solid
la **solution**	solution
la **somme**	sum (of money)

le **sommeil**	sleep
le **sommet**	summit (of mountain)
le **son**	sound
sonner	to ring
la **sonnerie**	ringing (of bells)
la **sorte**	sort
la **sortie**	exit
la **sortie de secours**	emergency exit
sortir	to go out
le **souci**	worry
la **soucoupe**	saucer
soudain	sudden; suddenly
souffler	to blow
souffrir	to suffer
souhaiter	to wish
soulager	to relieve
le **soulier**	shoe
soupçonner	to suspect
la **soupe**	soup
souper	to have supper
soupirer	to sigh
sourd	deaf
le **sourire**	smile
sourire	to smile
la **souris**	mouse
sous	under
le **sous-sol**	basement
le **sous-titre**	subtitle
le **soutien-gorge**	bra
le **souvenir**	memory

se **souvenir**	to remember
souvent	often
le **sparadrap**	plaster (for cuts)
la **spécialité**	speciality
le **spectacle**	show (entertainment)
le **sport**	sport
le **sport** d'hiver	winter sport
sportif (*m*)/**-ive** (*f*)	sporting
le **stade**	stadium
la **station**	station (underground)
la **station-service**	a service station
le **stationnement**	parking
stationner	to park
le **steak**	steak
le **stylo**	pen
le **sucre**	sugar
le **sud**	the south
ça **suffit**	that's enough
suggérer	to suggest
suisse/la **Suisse**	Swiss/Switzerland
tout de **suite**	immediately
suivant	following
suivre	to follow
au **sujet** de	about (concerning)
le **super**	petrol (high-octane)
supérieur	upper
le **supermarché**	supermarket
le **supplément**	supplement
supposer	to suppose

sur	on
sûr	sure
bien **sûr**	of course
surprenant	surprising
surtout	especially
sympa(tique)	nice (of people)
le **syndicat** d'initiative	tourist information office

_____   _____
_____   _____
_____   _____
_____   _____
_____   _____

ABCDEFGHIJKLMNOPQRS**T**UVWXYZ

le **tabac**	tobacco
la **table**	table
le **tableau**	picture
le **tableau** noir	backboard
le **tablier**	apron
le **tabouret**	stool
la **tache**	stain
la **tâche**	task
la **taille**	the waist
de grande **taille**	to be tall
tailler	to trim
se **taire**	to be quiet
le **talon**	heel

tandis que	whereas
tant	so much; so many
Tant mieux!	All the better!
Tant pis!	So much the worse! Too bad!
la **tante**	aunt
le **tapis**	carpet
tard	late (e.g. in the day)
le **tarif**	price list
la **tarte**	tart
la **tartine**	slice of bread and butter
le **tas**	heap
la **tasse**	cup
le **taureau**	bull
le **taux** (d'échange)	rate (of exchange)
le **taxe**	tax
tel (*m*)/**telle** (*f*)	such
le **télégramme**	telegram
le **téléphone**	telephone
téléphoner	to telephone
le **téléviseur**	television set
la **télévision**	television
tellement	so
le **témoin**	witness
la **température**	temperature
la **tempête**	storm
temporaire	temporary
le **temps**	the weather
de **temps** en temps	from time to time
mi- **temps**	half-time (e.g. in football)

tenir	to hold
le tennis	tennis
la tente	tent
terminer	to finish
le terrain de camping	camp-site
la terrasse	the pavement (outside cafe)
la terre	the earth
terrible	terrible
la tête	head
têtu	stubborn
le thé	tea
le théâtre	theatre
la théière	teapot
le ticket de quai	platform ticket
tiède	lukewarm
tiens!	well, well!
le timbre	stamp
timide	shy
le tire-bouchon	corkscrew
tirer	to pull
le tiroir	drawer
le titre	title
les toilettes (f)	toilets
le toit	roof
la tomate	tomato
tomber	to fall
la tonalité	tone (on phone)
tondre (la pelouse)	to mow (the lawn)
le tonnerre	thunder
le torchon	duster

tordre	to twist
avoir **tort**	to be wrong
la **tortue**	tortoise
tôt	early
toucher	to touch
toujours	still; always
le **tour**	circuit
la **tour**	tower
le **tourisme**	tourism
le/la **touriste**	tourist
le **tourne-disque**	record-player
tourner	to turn
tousser	to cough
tout à coup	suddenly
tout à fait	completely
tout à l'heure	just now
tout de même	all the same
tout de suite	immediately
tout droit	straight on
tout le monde	everybody
toutes directions	all traffic
traduire	to translate
le **train**	train
en **train** de	in the act of; in the middle of
traîner	to drag
le **trajet**	journey
la **tranche**	slice
tranquille	quiet
le **transistor**	transistor
le **travail**	work

travailler	to work
les travaux (*m*)	works
à travers	across
traverser	to cross
trembler	to tremble
tremper	to soak
très	very
tricher	to cheat
le tricot	jumper
tricoter	to knit
le trimestre	a term (e.g. at school)
triste	sad
se tromper	to make a mistake
trop	too
le trottoir	pavement
le trou	hole
trouver	to find
le truc	gadget
la truite	trout
le tube	tube
tuer	to kill
le type	chap
typique	typical

l'**uniforme** (*m*)	uniform
unique	unique; single
l'**université** (*f*)	university
urgent	urgent
usé	worn-out
l'**usine** (*f*)	factory
utile	useful
utiliser	to use

_____   _____
_____   _____
_____   _____
_____   _____
_____   _____

ABCDEFGHIJKLMNOPQRSTU**V**WXYZ

les **vacances** (*f*)	holidays
la **vache**	cow
la **vague**	wave
faire la **vaisselle**	to do the washing-up
valable	valid (e.g. a ticket)
la **valeur**	value
la **valise**	suitcase
la **vallée**	valley
valoir	to be worth
la **vanille**	vanilla
la **vapeur**	steam
le **vapeur**	steamship

varier	to vary
le **vase**	a vase
il **vaut** combien?	how much is it worth?
il **vaut** la peine	it is worthwhile
le **veau**	calf
la **vedette**	a star (e.g. of a film)
le **véhicule**	a vehicle
la **veille**	the day before
la **veille** de Noël	Christmas Eve
le **vélo**	bike
le **vélomoteur**	motorbike
la **vendange**	the grape harvest
le **vendeur**/la **vendeuse**	salesperson
vendre	to sell
venir	to come
venir de (faire)	to have just (done)
le **vent**	wind
en **vente**	on sale
le **ventre**	belly
le **ver**	worm
le **verger**	orchard
le **verglas**	ice (on roads)
vérifier	to check (e.g. oil)
la **vérité**	the truth
le **verre**	glass
vers	towards
verser	to pour
la **version**	version
version française	dubbed in French (film)

version originale	undubbed (film)
vert	green
la **veste**	jacket (short)
le **vestibule**	hall (in a house)
le **veston**	jacket (man's)
les **vêtements** (*m*)	clothes
le **veuf**	widower
la **veuve**	widow
la **viande**	meat
vide	empty
vider	to empty
la **vie**	life
le **vieillard**	an old man
vieux (*m*)/**vieille** (*f*)	old
vif (*m*)/**vive** (*f*)	alive
la **vigne**	vine
le **vignoble**	vineyard
le **village**	village
la **ville**	town
le **vin**	wine
la **vinaigre**	vinegar
la **violence**	violence
le **violon**	violin
le **virage**	bend (in the road)
le **visage**	face
la **visibilité**	visibility
la **visite**	visit
visiter	to visit
le **visiteur**/la **visiteuse**	visitor
vite	quickly
la **vitesse**	speed

première
vitesse (*f*) — first gear (e.g. in a car)

la **vitre** — window pane
la **vitrine** — shop window
vivement — briskly
vivre — to live
Tous mes
vœux! — All good wishes!

voici — here is; here are
la **voie** — track (at station)
voilà — there is, there are
le **voile** — veil (e.g. over face)
la **voile** — sail
voir — to see
le **voisin** /la **voisine** — neighbour
la **voiture** — car
la **voix** — voice
le **vol** — theft
le **volant** — steering wheel
voler — to fly
voler (quelque chose) — to steal (something)
le **volet** — shutter (on window)
le **voleur** — thief
volontiers — willingly
vomir — to vomit
vouloir — to want, to wish
vouloir dire — to mean
le **voyage** — journey
voyager — to travel
le **voyageur** — traveller
Voyons! — Let's see!

vrai	true
vraiment	truly
la **vue** (sur la mer)	view (over the sea)
avoir bonne **vue**	to have good eyesight

---

le **wagon**	carriage (on train)
le **wagon-lit**	sleeping car (on train)
le **wagon-restaurant**	dining car (on train)
les **W.C.** (*m*)	toilets
le **week-end**	weekend
le **western**	western (film)

---

y	there
le **yaourt**	yogurt
les **yeux** (*m*)	eyes

_____ _____
_____ _____
_____ _____
_____ _____
_____ _____

zéro	nought
la **zone**	zone
la **zone** piétonne	pedestrian zone
le **zoo**	zoo
Zut alors!	Gosh!

_____ _____
_____ _____
_____ _____
_____ _____

ENGLISH-FRENCH

to be **able**	pouvoir
about (approximately)	environ
about (concerning)	au sujet de
above	dessus
abroad	à l'étranger
absent	absent
absolutely	absolument
to **accelerate**	accélérer
accent	l'accent (*m*)
to **accept**	accepter, agréer
accident	l'accident (*m*)
to **accompany**	accompagner
accountant	le comptable
to **accuse**	accuser
across	à travers
in the **act** of	en train de
active	actif (*m*)/active (*f*)
actor	l'acteur (*m*)
actress	l'actrice (*f*)
address	l'adresse (*f*)
to **admire**	admirer
to **admit**	avouer
adorable	mignon (*m*)/ mignonne (*f*)
to **adore**	adorer
adult	l'adulte (*m or f*)
advertisement	l'annonce (*f*)
advertising	la publicité
to **advise**	conseiller
aeroplane	l'avion (*m*)
after	à partir de

again	encore; de nouveau
against	contre
air hostess	l'hôtesse de l'air (*f*)
airport	l'aéroport (*m*)
alarm clock	le réveil
Alas!	Hélas!
alive	vif (*m*), vive (*f*)
All the better!	Tant mieux!
all the same	quand même; tout de même
all traffic	toutes directions
to allow	permettre
almost	presque
alone	seul
along	le long de
already	déjà
also	aussi
always	toujours
American/America	américain/ l'Amérique (*f*)
among	parmi
amusing	amusant
angry	fâché
animal	la bête
annoyed	énervé
to answer	répondre
antiseptic	antiseptique
to apologize	s'excuser
apple	la pomme
to apply to	s'adresser
appointment (to meet)	le rendez-vous

approximately	à peu près
apricot	l'abricot (*m*)
apron	le tablier
arm (of the body)	le bras
armchair	le fauteuil
around	autour de
as much	autant
ashtray	un cendrier
to be ashamed	avoir honte
to ask (inquire)	demander
to ask (invite)	prier
to ask a question	poser une question
aspirin	l'aspirine (*f*)
to astonish	étonner
astonishing	étonnant
atmosphere	l'ambiance (*f*)
attack of nerves	la crise de nerfs
attendant (in a museum)	le gardien
attic	le grenier
aunt	la tante
avenue	le boulevard

baby	le bébé
back (part of body)	le dos
bad	mauvais
bag	le sac
baker	le boulanger
bakery	la boulangerie
ball	le ballon
banana	la banane
to bandage	panser
bank (e.g. in the High Street)	la banque
bank (of river)	la rive
banker's card	la carte bancaire
banknote	le billet de banque
bar (selling drinks)	le bistro
bare	nu
to bark	aboyer
barmaid	la serveuse
barman	le serveur
basement	le sous-sol
basket	le panier
bath	le bain
bathroom	la salle de bains
bath (tub)	la baignoire
to bathe	se baigner
bathing costume	le maillot de bain
battery (small)	la pile
to be able	pouvoir
to be present at	assister à
to be quiet	se taire
to be right	avoir raison

to be sorry	regretter
to be tall	être de grande taille
to be worth	valoir
to be wrong	avoir tort
beach	la plage
beans	les haricots (*m*)
bear	l'ours (*m*)
beautiful	beau (*m*)/belle (*f*)
because	parce que
because of	à cause de
to become	devenir
bed	le lit
bedroom	la chambre
bee	l'abeille (*f*)
beer	la bière
to begin	commencer
beginning	le début
on behalf of	de la part de
behind	derrière
Belgian/Belgium	belge/la Belgique
to believe	croire
bell	la cloche
belly	le ventre
below	dessous
bench	un banc
bend (in the road)	un virage
beside	à côté de
better; best (*adv*)	mieux
better; best (*adj*)	meilleur
between	entre
bicycle	la bicyclette

big	gros (*m*)/grosse (*f*)
bike	le vélo
bike-ride	la promenade à velo
the bill (e.g. in a café)	l'addition (*f*)
bin	la poubelle
biology	la biologie
bird	l'oiseau (*m*)
birth	la naissance
to bite	mordre
black	noir
blackboard	le tableau noir
blanket	la couverture
block of flats	l'immeuble (*m*)
blood	le sang
blouse	le chemisier
to blow	souffler
to blow up (a tyre)	gonfler
blue	bleu
on board (ship)	à bord
to board (a ship)	embarquer
board and lodging	la pension complète
boat	le bateau
body	le corps
bone	l'os (*m*)
book	le livre
bookshop	la librairie
to be bored	s'ennuyer
boring	ennuyeux (*m*)/ ennuyeuse (*f*)
born	né
to be born	naître

to **borrow**	emprunter
boss	le patron
bottle	la bouteille
bottom (e.g. of a well)	le fond
bowl	le bol
bowls	les boules (f)
box	la boîte
boy	le garçon
bra	le soutien-gorge
brake	le frein
to **brake**	freiner
bread	le pain
slice of **bread** and butter	la tartine
to **break**	casser
breakdown	la panne
breakfast	le petit déjeuner
break-time (at school)	la récreation
out of **breath**	essoufflé
to **breathe**	respirer
bridge	le pont
brief	bref (m)/brève (f)
to **bring**	amener; apporter
to **bring** back	ramener; rapporter
briskly	vivement
British	britannique
broadcast	l'émission (f)
broken-down (of cars)	en panne
brother	le frère
brown	brun
brown (chestnut)	marron

brush	la brosse
to brush yourself	se brosser
bucket	le seau
to build	bâtir; construire
building	le bâtiment
bulb (electric)	l'ampoule (*f*)
bull	le taureau
bullock	le bœuf
burglar	le cambrioleur
to burn	brûler
bus	l'autobus (*m*)
bus station	la gare routière
bus stop	l'arrêt d'autobus (*m*)
bush	le buisson
business	les affaires (*f*)
busy	occupé
but	mais
butcher	le boucher
butcher's shop	la boucherie
butter	le beurre
butterfly	le papillon
button	le bouton
to buy	acheter

_____   _____

_____   _____

_____   _____

_____   _____

_____   _____

cabbage	le chou
cake	le gâteau
cake shop	la pâtisserie
calf	le veau
to **call** the police	appeler police secours
calm	calme
camera	l'appareil-photo (*m*)
to **camp**	camper
camper	le campeur
camp site	le terrain de camping
Canada	le Canada
Canadian	canadien (*m*)/ canadienne (*f*)
capital letter	la majuscule
car	la voiture
caravan	la caravane
care (e.g. of children)	le soin
career	la carrière
careful	prudent
to be **careful**	faire attention
caretaker	le/la concierge
car park	le parking
carpet	le tapis
carriage (on train)	le wagon
carrot	la carotte
to **carry**	porter
cartoon	la bande dessinée
in that **case**	dans ce cas
cash desk	la caisse

castle	le château
cat	le chat
to catch	attraper
cathedral	la cathédrale
cauliflower	le chou-fleur
ceiling	le plafond
to celebrate	fêter
cellar	la cave
central heating	le chauffage central
centre	le centre
century	le siècle
certainly	certainement
chair	la chaise
championship	le championnat
change	le changement
change (i.e. small change)	la monnaie
to change	changer
channel (on TV)	la chaîne
the Channel (English)	la Manche
chap	le type
charming	charmant
to chat	causer
to chatter	bavarder
cheap	bon marché
to cheat	tricher
to check (e.g. oil)	vérifier
to check (tickets)	contrôler
cheese	le fromage
chemist	le pharmacien
chemistry	la chimie
chemist's	la pharmacie

cheque-book	le carnet de chèques
cherry	la cerise
chess	les échecs (*m*)
chest (part of body)	la poitrine
chicken	le poulet
chief	le chef
child	l'enfant (*m* or *f*)
chin	le menton
chips	les frites (*f*)
chocolate	le chocolat
choice	le choix
to choose	choisir
chop (e.g. pork)	la côtelette
Christmas	Noël (*m*)
Christmas Eve	la veille de Noël
church	l'église (*f*)
cider	le cidre
cinema	le cinéma
circuit	le tour
civil servant	le/la fonctionnaire
clean	propre
to clean	nettoyer
clear	clair
clever	habile
cliff	la falaise
climate	le climat
to climb	grimper
clock	l'horloge (*f*); la pendule
to close	fermer
clothes	les vêtements (*m*)

cloud	le nuage
cloudy	nuageux (*m*)/ -euse (*f*)
clutch (on a car)	l'embrayage (*m*)
coach (vehicle)	l'autocar (*m*)
coal	le charbon
coast	une côte
coat	le manteau
coffee	le café
coffee with milk (large)	le café au lait
coffee with milk (small)	le café crème
coffee-pot	la cafetière
cold (the illness)	le rhume
cold	froid
to be cold	avoir froid
to collect	collectionner
collection (of mail)	la levée
collision	la collision
colour	la couleur
comb	le peigne
to comb your hair	se peigner
to come	venir
comfort	le confort
comfortable	confortable
coming from (e.g. a train)	en provenance de
company (in business)	la société
compartment (in a train)	le compartiment
competition	le concours
to complain	se plaindre
complaint	la réclamation
completely	tout à fait

compulsory	obligatoire
computer	l'ordinateur (*m*)
to **concern**	s'agir de
concert	le concert
to **congratulate**	féliciter
congratulations	félicitations (*f*)
connection (e.g. a train)	la correspondance
to **continue**	continuer
on the **contrary**	au contraire
to **cook**	cuire
cooker	la cuisinière
cool	frais (*m*)/fraîche (*f*)
corkscrew	le tire-bouchon
corner	le coin
correct	exact; juste
to **correct**	corriger
corridor	le couloir
to **cost**	coûter
cotton wool	le coton hydrophile; l'ouate hydrophile (*f*)
to **cough**	tousser
to **count**	compter
country	le pays
countryside	la campagne
country	le département
course (at dinner)	le plat
of **course**	bien entendu; bien sûr
cousin	le cousin/la cousine
to **cover**	couvrir

cow	la vache
crab	le crabe
credit card	la carte de crédit
to cross	traverser
crossroads	le carrefour
crowd	la foule
to crush	écraser
to cry	pleurer
cucumber	le concombre
cup	la tasse
cupboard	le placard
to cure	guérir
curtain	le rideau
cushion	le coussin
customer	le client
customs	la douane
customs officer	le douanier
to cut	couper
cyclist	le/la cycliste

_____   _____
_____   _____
_____   _____
_____   _____
_____   _____

daily	quotidien (*m*)/ -ienne (*f*)
dairy	une crémerie
damp	humide
dance (that you go to)	le bal
to **dance**	danser
dangerous	dangereux (*m*)/-euse (*f*)
to **dare**	oser
dark (colour)	foncé
date	la date
daughter	la fille
day	la journée
the **day** after tomorrow	après-demain
the **day** before	la veille
the **day** before yesterday	avant-hier
dead	mort
deaf	sourd
dear	cher (*m*)/chère (*f*)
to **decide** to	décider de
deep	profound
delighted	ravi
demonstration	la manifestation
dentist	le/la dentiste
to **deny**	nier
department (in a store)	le rayon
departure	le départ
it **depends**	ça dépend
to **describe**	décrire
desire	l'envie (*f*)
despite	malgré
dessert	le dessert

detour	la déviation
to dial	composer
diarrhoea	la diarrhée
to die	mourir
difficult	difficile
to dine	dîner
dining car (on train)	le wagon-restaurant
dining-room	la salle à manger
dirty	sale
to disappear	disparaître
disappointed	déçu
disco	la disco
to discover	découvrir
to discuss	discuter
disgusting	dégoûtant
dishwasher	le lave-vaisselle
district	le quartier
to disturb	déranger
to dive	plonger
divorced	divorcé
to do	faire
to do the shopping	faire les courses
do-it-yourself	le bricolage
doctor	le docteur; le médecin
dog	le chien
done to a turn (meat)	à point
don't mention it	je t'en (vous en) prie
door	la porte
door (of vehicle)	la portière
dormitory	le dortoir

without **doubt**	sans doute
double sink unit	l'évier à deux bacs
downstairs	en bas
dozen	la douzaine
to **drag**	traîner
drawer	le tiroir
drawing	le dessin
drawing-room	le salon
to **dream**	rêver
dress	la robe
to **dress** yourself	s'habiller
dressing (e.g. on a wound)	le pansement
drink	la boisson
to **drink**	boire
drinkable	potable
to **drive** (vehicle)	conduire
to **drive** along (travel)	rouler
driver	le chauffeur; le conducteur
driving licence	le permis de conduire
drop (e.g. of water)	une goutte
to **drop**	laisser tomber
to **drown**	se noyer
dry	sec (*m*)/sèche (*f*)
dry-cleaning	le nettoyage à sec
dubbed in French (film)	version française
duck	le canard
duration	la durée
during	pendant
dust	la poussière

duster	le torchon
Dutch	hollandais

_____   _____
_____   _____
_____   _____
_____   _____

each	chaque
each one	chacun (*m*)/ chacune (*f*)
ear	l'oreille (*f*)
early	de bonne heure; tôt
to earn (e.g. money)	gagner
the earth	la terre
Easter	Pâques (*f*)
easy	facile
to eat	manger
at the edge of	au bord de
education	l'enseignement (*m*)
egg	l'œuf (*m*)
electrician	l'électricien
electricity	l'électricité (*f*)
elsewhere	ailleurs
emergency exit	la sortie de secours
employee	l'employé (*m*)/ l'employée (*f*)

empty	vide
to empty	vider
end	la fin
at the end of	au bout de
engagement (to be wed)	les fiançailles (*f*)
engine	le moteur
engineer	l'ingénieur (*m*)
English/England	anglais/l'Angleterre (*f*)
enormous	énorme
enough	assez
that's enough	ça suffit
to enter	entrer
entire	entier (*m*)/entière (*f*)
entrance	l'entrée (*f*)
envelope	l'enveloppe (*f*)
equal	égal
escalator	l'escalier roulant (*m*)
especially	surtout
essential	essentiel (*m*)/-ielle (*f*)
European	européen (*m*)/européenne (*f*)
even	même
evening	le soir
event	l'événement (*m*)
everybody	tout le monde
everywhere	partout
evidently	évidemment
to exaggerate	exagérer
exam	un examen

exam (pre-university)	le bac(calauréat)
for **example**	par exemple
except	sauf
exchange	l'échange (*f*)
to **exchange**	échanger
exchange office	le bureau de change
exciting	passionnant
Excuse me!	Pardon!
exercise book	le cahier
exit	la sortie
to **explain**	expliquer
extremely	extrêmement
eye	l'œil (*m*)
eyes	les yeux (*m*)

———————————————   ———————————————

———————————————   ———————————————

———————————————   ———————————————

———————————————   ———————————————

———————————————————————————

face	la figure; le visage
in **fact**	en effet
factory	l'usine (*f*)
to **fail**	échouer
to **fail** (e.g. an exam)	rater
to **faint**	s'évanouir
fair	la foire

to **fall**	tomber
to **fall** asleep	s'endormir
false	faux (*m*)/fausse (*f*)
family	la famille
famous	célèbre
far	loin
farm	la ferme
fashion	la mode
fast	rapide
fat	gras (*m*)/grasse (*f*)
father	le père
father-in-law	le beau-père
favourite	favori (*m*)/-ite (*f*)
fear	la peur
to be **fed up**	en avoir marre
to **feed**	nourrir
to **feel**	sentir
ferry	le ferry
field	le champ
to **fight**	se battre
to **fill**	remplir
to **fill up** (with petrol)	faire le plein
film (for a camera)	la pellicule
finally	enfin; finalement
to **find**	trouver
to **find** oneself	se rencontrer
fine	l'amende (*f*)
finger	le doigt
to **finish**	finir; terminer
fire	le feu
fire (e.g. in a building)	l'incendie (*m*)

fireman	le pompier
first	premier (*m*)/ première (*f*)
first name	le prénom
first of all	d'abord
fish	le poisson
to **fish**	pêcher
to go **fishing**	faire la pêche
fishing-rod	la canne à pêche
flag	le drapeau
flat (i.e. an apartment)	l'appartement (*m*)
floor (of room)	le plancher
floor (storey)	l'étage (*m*)
flour	la farine
flower	la fleur
fly	la mouche
to **fly**	voler
fog	le brouillard
to **follow**	suivre
following	suivant
food	la nourriture
foot	le pied
football	le football
for	pour
for (because)	car
to **forbid**	interdire
it is **forbidden** to …	Défense de … Interdit de …
foreigner	l'étranger (*m*)/ l'étrangère (*f*)
to **foresee**	prévoir

forest	la forêt
to forget	oublier
to forgive	pardonner
fork (cutlery)	la fourchette
form (to fill in)	la fiche
fortnight	la quinzaine
fortunately	heureusement
fox	le renard
fragile	fragile
frank	franc (*m*)/franche (*f*)
frankly	franchement
free	libre
free (no charge)	gratuit
to freeze	geler
freezer	le congélateur
fridge	le frigo
French/France	français/la France
fridge	le frigo
friend	l'ami (*m*)/l'amie (*f*); le/la camarade; le copain/la copine
friendship	l'amitié (*f*)
fright	l'épouvante (*f*)
to be frightened	avoir peur
frightful	affreux (*m*)/affreuse (*f*)
frog	la grenouille
in front of	devant
frontier	la frontière
fruit	le fruit

fruit juice	le jus de fruit
fruit-seller	le marchand de fruits
frying-pan	la poêle
full (bus, hotel)	complet (*m*)/ complète (*f*)
full (container)	plein
to function	fonctionner
funny	drôle
furious	furieux (*m*)/-ieuse (*f*)
furnished	meublé
furniture	les meubles (*m*)
future	l'avenir (*m*)

_____   _____
_____   _____
_____   _____
_____   _____

_____

ABCDEF**G**HIJKLMNOPQRSTUVWXYZ

gadget	le truc
game	le jeu
garage	le garage
garden	le jardin
gardening	le jardinage
garlic	l'ail (*m*)
gas	le gaz
gate	la barrière

to **gather**	ramasser
first **gear** (e.g. in a car)	première vitesse (*f*)
in **general**	en général
generally	généralement
generous	généreux (*m*)/ généreuse (*f*)
gently	doucement
geography	la géographie
German/Germany	allemand/ l'Allemagne (*f*)
to **get** angry	se mettre en colère
to **get** lost	se perdre
to **get** up	se lever
girl	la jeune fille
to **give**	donner
to **give** back	rendre
glass	le verre
glasses (spectacles)	les lunettes (*f*)
glove	le gant
to **go**	aller
to **go** away	s'éloigner
to **go** camping	faire du camping
to **go** down	descendre
to **go** for a walk	se promener
to **go** out	sortir
to **go** to bed	se coucher
to **go** up	monter
goal	le but
God	Dieu (*m*)
gold	l'or (*m*)
Good heavens!	Oh là là!

goodbye	au revoir
goose	l'oie (*f*)
Gosh!	Zut alors!
government	le gouvernement
gram(me)	le gramme
granddaughter	la petite-fille
grandfather	le grand-père
grandmother	la grand-mère
grandson	le petit-fils
grape	le raisin
grape harvest	la vendange
grass	l'herbe (*f*)
grateful	reconnaissant
gravy	la sauce
Great Britain	la Grande-Bretagne
Greece	la Grèce
Greek	grec (*m*)/grecque (*f*)
green	vert
greengrocer	le marchand de légumes
to greet	saluer
grey	gris
grocer	l'épicier (*m*)
grocer's shop	l'épicerie (*f*); l'alimentation (*f*)
ground	le sol
ground floor	le rez-de-chaussée
group	le groupe
to grow (e.g. plants)	cultiver
to guarantee	garantir
guide	le guide

guitar	la guitare
gymnastics	la gymnastique

----

hail (frozen rain)	la grêle
hair	les cheveux (*m*)
hairdresser	le coiffeur
hair-dryer	le sèche-cheveux
half	demi
half	la moitié
half-board	demi-pension (*f*)
half-time (e.g. in football)	mi-temps
hall (in a house)	le vestibule
ham	le jambon
hand	la main
handbag	le sac à main
handkerchief	le mouchoir
to happen	se passer
happy	heureux (*m*)/-reuse (*f*); gai; content
Happy New Year!	Bonne Année!
hard	dur
in haste	à la hâte

hat	le chapeau
to hate	détester
to have a good time	s'amuser
to have good eyesight	avoir bonne vue
to have just (done)	venir de (faire)
to have supper	souper
to have to	devoir
having a cold	enrhumé
head	tête
to head for	se diriger vers
headache	le mal de tête
to have a headache	avoir mal à la tête
headlight	le phare
headmaster/mistress	le directeur/la directrice
health	la santé
healthy	sain
heap	le tas
to hear	entendre
heart	le cœur
heat	la chaleur
heavy	lourd
heel	le talon
Hello!	Salut!
to help	aider
help	le secours
helping hand	le coup de main
hen	la poule
here	ici
here is; here are	voici

to **hesitate**	hésiter
to **hide**	cacher
the **highway** code	le code de la route
hill	la colline
to **hire**	louer
hiring	la location
history	l'histoire (f)
to **hit**	frapper
hitch-hiking	l'autostop (m)
hobby	le passe-temps
hockey	le hockey
to **hold**	tenir
hole	le trou
holiday (public)	la fête
on **holiday**	en congé
holidays	les vacances (f)
Holland	l'Hollande (f)
at the **home** of	chez
homework	les devoirs (m)
honest	honnête
honey	le miel
hope	l'espoir (m)
to **hope**	espérer
horse	le cheval
horse-riding	l'équitation (f)
hospital	l'hôpital (m)
hospitality	l'hospitalité (f)
hot	chaud
to be **hot**	avoir chaud
hotel	l'hôtel (m)
house	la maison

to do the	
housework	faire le ménage
hovercraft	l'aéroglisseur (*m*)
how	comment
how much, how many	combien
how much is it worth?	il vaut combien?
however	cependant, pourtant
to be **hungry**	avoir faim
hunting	la chasse
to **hurry**	se dépêcher
in a **hurry**	pressé
husband	l'époux (*m*); le mari
hypermarket	l'hypermarché (*m*)

_____   _____
_____   _____
_____   _____
_____   _____

ABCDEFGH**I**JKLMNOPQRSTUVWXYZ

ice (-cream)	la glace
ice (on roads)	le verglas
idea	l'idée (*f*)
identification	la pièce d'identité
if	si
to be **ignorant** of	ignorer
illness	la maladie
immediately	immédiatement; tout de suite

immense	immense
to impede	gêner
important	important
impossible	impossible
impression	l'impression (f)
impressive	impressionnant
to improve	améliorer
included	compris
to increase	augmenter
incredible	incroyable
indigestion	l'indigestion (f)
industrial	industriel (m)/-ielle (f)
industry	l'industrie (f)
influenza	la grippe
to inform	informer
information	l'information (f); les renseignements (m)
information office	le bureau de renseignements
tourist information office	le syndicat d'initiative
inhabitant	l'habitant (m)
injured	blessé
insect	l'insect (m)
to insert (e.g. a coin)	introduire
inside	dedans; là-dedans
instant	l'instant (m)
instead of	au lieu de
instrument	l'instrument (m)
to insult	insulter

intelligent	intelligent
intention	l'intention (*f*)
interest	l'intérêt (*m*)
to be **interested** in	s'intéresser à
interesting	intéressant
interview	l'entrevue (*f*)
to **introduce** (a person)	présenter
invitation	l'invitation (*f*)
to **invite**	inviter
invoice	la facture
Irish/Ireland	irlandais/l'Irlande (*f*)
to **iron** (clothes)	repasser
island	l'île (*f*)
Italian	italien (*m*)/-ienne (*f*)
Italy	l'Italie (*f*)

_____   _____

_____   _____

_____   _____

_____   _____

ABCDEFGHIJKLMNOPQRSTUVWXYZ

jacket (short)	la veste
jacket (man's)	le veston
jam	la confiture
jealous	jaloux (*m*)/jalouse (*f*)

jeans	le jean
jewel	le bijou
job (employment; post)	l'emploi
job (trade; profession)	le métier
joke	la blague; la plaisanterie
journey	le trajet; le voyage
to **judge**	juger
to **jump**	sauter
jumper	le tricot
just now	tout à l'heure

_____   _____
_____   _____
_____   _____
_____   _____

to **keep**	garder
key	la clé/la clef
to **kill**	tuer
kilogram(me)	le kilo
kilometre	le kilomètre
king	le roi
kiosk	le kiosque
kiss	la bise
to **kiss**	embrasser
kitchen	la cuisine

knee	le genou
knife	le couteau
to knit	tricoter
to knock against	se heurter
to knock over	renverser
to know (a person or a place)	connaître
to know (a thing)	savoir

_____ _____
_____ _____
_____ _____
_____ _____

ABCDEFGHIJK**L**MNOPQRSTUVWXYZ

laboratory	le laboratoire
lack	la faute
ladder	l'échelle (*f*)
lady	la dame
lake	le lac
lamb	l'agneau (*m*)
lamp	la lampe
to land (e.g. a plane)	atterrir
landing (upstairs)	le palier
landscape	le paysage
language	la langue
last	dernier (*m*)/dernière (*f*)
to last	durer

late (behind schedule)	en retard
late (e.g. in the day)	tard
to laugh	rire
launderette	la laverie automatique
law	la loi
lawn	la pelouse
lawyer	l'avocat (*m*)
to lay the table	mettre le couvert
lazy	paresseux (*m*)/-euse (*f*)
to lead	mener
leak (water)	la fuite d'eau
to lean	pencher
to learn	apprendre
leather	le cuir
to leave	partir
to leave (a place)	quitter
leek	le poireau
to the left	à gauche
left-luggage office	la consigne
leg	la jambe
lemon	le citron
lemonade	la limonade
to lend	prêter
less	moins
lesson	la leçon
to let	laisser
Let's see!	Voyons!
letter	la lettre
letter-box	la boîte aux lettres

lettuce	la laitue
level	le niveau
level crossing	le passage à niveau
liberty	la liberté
library	la bibliothèque
to lie (to tell untruths)	mentir
life	la vie
lift	l'ascenseur (*m*)
to lift (phone receiver)	décrocher
light	la lumière
light (i.e. not heavy)	léger (*m*)/légère (*f*)
to light	allumer
lighter (cigarettes)	le briquet
like	comme
to like	aimer
likeable	aimable
line	la ligne
lip	la lèvre
list	la liste
to listen	écouter
litre	le litre
little	un peu
to live	vivre
to live (reside)	demeurer; habiter
loaf	la baguette
to lodge	loger
a long time	longtemps
to look	regarder
to look after	soigner
to look for	chercher
to look like	ressembler

lorry	le camion
lorry (large)	le poids lourd
to **lose**	perdre
loss	la perte
lost property	les objets trouvés (*m*)
lost-property office	le bureau des objets trouvés
a **lot**	beaucoup
lounge	la salle de séjour
love	l'amour (*m*)
luck	la chance
luggage	les bagages (*m*)
lukewarm	tiède
to **lunch**	déjeuner
luxury	le luxe

_____   _____
_____   _____
_____   _____
_____   _____

ABCDEFGHIJKL**M**NOPQRSTUVWXYZ

mad	fou (*m*)/folle (*f*)
magazine	la magazine; la revue
magazine (weekly)	l'hebdomadaire (*m*)
magnificent	magnifique

mail	le courrier
make (e.g. of car)	la marque
to **make** a mistake	se tromper
to **make** the acquaintance of	faire la connaissance de
make-up	le maquillage
man	l'homme (*m*)
manner	la manière
map (of roads)	la carte routière
map (of town)	le plan
mark (e.g. in an exam)	la note
market	le marché
to **marry**	épouser; se marier avec
marvellous	merveilleux (*m*)/ -euse (*f*); formid- able
master	le maître
match (e.g. football)	le match
match (e.g. for fire)	l'allumette (*f*)
maths	les mathématiques (*f*)
it doesn't **matter**	n'importe
mattress	le matelas
mayor	le maire
meadow	le pré
meal	le repas
to **mean**	vouloir dire
meat	la viande
mechanic	le garagiste, le mécanicien

medicine	le médicament
to meet	rencontrer
to meet (two people or things)	se rencontrer
meeting	la réunion
member	le membre
memory	le souvenir
to mend	raccommoder
Don't mention it!	De rien!
menu	le menu
message	le message
metal	le métal
metre	le mètre
microcomputer	le micro-ordinateur
midday	midi
in the middle of	au milieu de
midnight	minuit (*f*)
milk	le lait
million	le million
minute	la minute
mirror	le miroir
mirror (in a vehicle)	le rétroviseur
to miss (e.g. the train)	manquer
mist	la brume
mistake	l'erreur (*f*)
mistress	la maîtresse
modern	moderne
moment	le moment
money	l'argent (*m*)
monument	le monument
moon	la lune
more	plus

morning	le matin
most	la plupart
mother	la mère
mother-in-law	la belle-mère
motionless	immobile
motorbike	le vélomoteur; la moto
motorway	l'autoroute (*f*)
mountain	la montagne
mountaineering	l'alpinisme (*m*)
mouse	la souris
mouth	la bouche
to move	bouger
to move back	reculer
to move house	déménager
movement	le mouvement
to mow (the lawn)	tondre (la pelouse)
museum	le musée
mushroom	le champignon
music	la musique
musician	le musicien
mussels	les moules (*f*)
mustard	la moutarde

nail (e.g. a toe-nail)	l'ongle (*m*)
name	le nom
narrow	étroit
nasty	méchant
natural	naturel (*m*)/ naturelle (*f*)
naturally	naturellement
near to	près de
near	proche
necessary	nécessaire
to be necessary	falloir
it is necessary	il faut
neck	le cou
to need	avoir besoin de
need	un besoin
neighbour	le voisin /la voisine
neither	non plus
neither ... nor ...	ne ... ni ... ni ...
nephew	le neveu
nervous	nerveux (*m*)/-euse (*f*)
nest	le nid
net	le filet
the Netherlands	l'Hollande (*f*)
never	ne ... jamais
nevertheless	néanmoins
new	nouveau (*m*)/-elle (*f*)
new (newly manufactured)	neuf (*m*)/neuve (*f*)
the news	les actualités (*f*)
news (an item of)	la nouvelle (*f*)
news (e.g. on TV)	les informations (*f*)
newspaper	un journal

next	prochain
the next day	le lendemain
nice	gentil (*m*)/-tille (*f*); chouette
nice (of people)	sympa(thique)
niece	la nièce
night	la nuit
no	aucun
No entry	Sens interdit (*m*)
no longer	ne … plus
nobody	ne … personne
noise	le bruit
noisy	bruyant
normally	normalement
the north	le nord
nose	le nez
not	ne … pas
not at all	pas du tout
not included	non compris
nothing	ne … rien
to notice	remarquer
nought	zéro
novel	le roman
now	maintenant
number (amount)	le nombre
number (house, page)	le numéro
number plate	la plaque d'immatriculation
numerous	nombreux (*m*)/-euse (*f*)
nurse	l'infirmière (*f*)
nylon	le nylon

to obey	obéir
to oblige	obliger
ocean	l'océan (*m*)
of course	bien sûr
offer	l'offre (*f*)
to offer	offrir
oil	l'huile (*f*)
okay!	d'accord
old	vieux (*m*)/vieille (*f*)
older	aîné
old man	le vieillard
omelette	l'omelette (*f*)
on	sur
once	une fois
one-way system	sens unique (*m*)
onion	l'oignon (*m*)
only	ne … que, seulement
open	ouvert
to open	ouvrir
in the open air	en plein air
opera	l'opéra (*m*)
operation	l'opération (*f*)
opinion	l'opinion (*f*)
in my opinion	à mon avis
opportunity	l'occasion (*f*)
opposite	en face de
optician	l'opticien (*m*)
or	ou
orange	l'orange (*f*)
orchard	le verger
orchestra	l'orchestre (*m*)
order	l'ordre (*m*)

to **order** (e.g. a meal)	commander
ordinary	ordinaire
to **organize**	organiser
otherwise	autrement
our	notre (*s*)/nos (*pl*)
outside	dehors
oven	le four
over there	là-bas
overcoat	le pardessus
to **overtake**	doubler
owner	le/la propriétaire
oyster	l'huître (*f*)

_____   _____
_____   _____
_____   _____
_____   _____

ABCDEFGHIJKLMNO**P**QRSTUVWXYZ

page (of book)	la page
pain	la douleur
painting	la peinture
pair	le paire
palace	le palais
pale	pâle
pancake	la crêpe
paper	le papier
parcel	le colis; le paquet

parents	les parents (*m*)
Parisian	parisien (*m*)/ -ienne (*f*)
park	un parc
to **park**	stationner; garer
parking	le stationnement
part (of a whole)	la partie
in **particular**	en particulier
party	la boum
party (more formal)	la soirée
passenger	le passager
passer-by	le passant
passport	le passeport
in the **past**	autrefois
path	le sentier
patient	patient
pavement	le trottoir
pavement (outside café)	la terrasse
to **pay**	payer
payment	le paiement
pea	le pois; le petit pois
peach	la pêche
pear	la poire
peasant	le paysan
pedestrian crossing	le passage clouté
pedestrian	le piéton
pedestrian zone	la zone piétonne
to **peel**	éplucher
pen	le stylo
pen-friend	le correspondant/ la correspondante

penknife	le canif
pencil	le crayon
people	les gens (*m*)
pepper	le poivre
per cent	pour cent
per day	par jour
perfect	parfait
perfectly	parfaitement
performance (at cinema)	la séance
perfume	le parfum
perhaps	peut-être
period (of time)	l'époque (*f*)
permanent	permanent
person	la personne
petrol	l'essence (*f*)
petrol (high-octane)	le super
petrol-pump attendant	le/la pompiste
photo	la photo
photographer	le/la photographe
photography	la photographie
piano	le piano
picnic	le pique-nique
picture	le tableau
picture (e.g. in a book)	l'image (*f*)
picturesque	pittoresque
piece	le morceau
pig	le cochon; le porc
pill	la pilule
pillow	l'oreiller (*m*)
pilot	le pilote
pineapple	l'ananas (*m*)

pitch (e.g. on camp-site)	l'emplacement (*m*)
What a **pity**!	Quel dommage!
place	le lieu; l'endroit (*m*)
plan (e.g. for future)	le projet
plant	la plante
plaster (for cuts)	le sparadrap
plate	l'assiette (*f*)
platform (at station)	le quai
platform ticket	le ticket de quai
play (e.g. at a theatre)	la pièce de théâtre
to **play**	jouer
player	le joueur
playground	la cour
pleasant	agréable
please	s'il te (vous) plaît
to **please**	plaire
pleased to meet you	enchanté
pleasure	le plaisir
plum	la prune
plumber	le plombier
pocket	la poche
point	le point
to **point** to	indiquer
the **police**	la police
policeman	le gendarme; l'agent de police (*m*)
policeman (slang)	un flic
police station	un commissariat
polite	poli
politeness	la politesse
pollution	la pollution

poor	pauvre
pork-butcher's	la charcuterie
port	le port
porter	le porteur
to post (a letter)	poster; mettre à la poste
postcard	la carte postale
poster	l'affiche (*f*)
postman	le facteur
post office	le bureau de poste
pot	le pot
potato	la pomme de terre
pound (money)	la livre sterling
pound (weight)	la livre
to pour	verser
to practise	pratiquer
precious	précieux (*m*)/ -ieuse (*f*)
to prefer	préférer
to prepare	préparer
prescription	l'ordonnance (*f*)
at present	actuellement
present (e.g. birthday)	le cadeau
present (here, now)	présent
to be present	assister à
to press	appuyer
pressure	la pression
pretty	joli
to prevent	empêcher
price	le prix
price list	le tarif

priest	le curé
Prime Minister	le Premier Ministre
private	privé
probable	probable
problem	le problème
profession	la profession
programme (e.g. TV)	le programme
progress	le progrès
to promise	promettre
to pronounce	prononcer
to protect	protéger
to protest	protester
proud	fier (*m*)/fière (*f*)
to prove	prouver
public	public (*m*)/ publique (*f*)
public holiday	le jour férié
to pull	tirer
pullover	le pull(-over)
punctured	crevé
to punish	punir
pupil	l'élève (*m or f*)
purchase	l'achat (*m*)
pure	pur
on purpose	exprès
purse	le porte-monnaie
to push	pousser
to put	mettre
to put out (a light)	éteindre
to put someone up	héberger
pyjamas	le pyjama

quality	la qualité
quantity	la quantité
quarter	le quart
queen	la reine
question	la question
to queue	faire la queue
quickly	vite; rapidement
quiet	tranquille

_____   _____

_____   _____

_____   _____

_____   _____

ABCDEFGHIJKLMNOPQ**R**STUVWXYZ

rabbit	le lapin
radiator	le radiateur
radio	la radio
railway	le chemin de fer
rain	la pluie
to rain (heavily)	pleuvoir (à verse)
raincoat	l'imperméable (*m*)
rainy	pluvieux (*m*)/ -ieuse (*f*)
rare (of steaks)	saignant
rarely	rarement
raspberry	la framboise
rate (of exchange)	le taux (d'échange)

rather	plutôt
razor	le rasoir
to read	lire
reading	la lecture
ready	prêt
to realize	se rendre compte
really	en réalité
reason	la raison
receipt	le reçu
to receive	recevoir
receiver (phone)	le recepteur
recent	récent
recently	récemment
reception desk	la réception
recipe	la recette
to recognize	reconnaître
to recommend	recommander
record	le disque
record-player	le tourne-disque
to recover (from illness)	se remettre
red	rouge
red (e.g. hair)	roux (m)/rousse (f)
reduction	la réduction
referee	l'arbitre (m)
to refuse	refuser
region	la région
regular	régulier (m)/-ière (f)
regulation	le règlement
to relieve	soulager
remedy	le remède
to remember	se rappeler; se souvenir

to **remind**	rappeler
to **remove**	enlever; ôter
rent	le loyer
repair	la réparation
to **repair**	réparer
to **repair** (a car)	dépanner
to **repay**	rembourser
to **repeat**	répéter
reservation	la réservation
to **reserve**	réserver
to **reside**	demeurer; habiter
residence	le domicile
responsible	responsable
to **rest**	se reposer
restaurant	le restaurant
result	le résultat
return	le retour
return (to school)	la rentrée
to **return**	retourner; revenir
to **return** (e.g. home)	rentrer
return ticket	l'aller-retour (*m*)
reward	la récompense
ribbon	le ruban
rice	le riz
rich	riche
rifle	le fusil
on the **right**	à droite
to be **right**	avoir raison
ring (e.g. on a finger)	la bague
to **ring**	sonner
to **ring** off (on phone)	raccrocher

ringing (of bells)	la sonnerie
risk	le risque
river	la rivière
river (large)	le fleuve
road (main)	la route
roadway	la chaussée
roast	rôti
roof	le toit
room	la pièce
rose	la rose
round	rond
roundabout (traffic)	le rond-point
rubber	la gomme
rucksack	le sac à dos
rude	impoli
rugby	le rugby
rule(r)	la règle
to **run**	courir
to **run** away	se sauver
to **run** errands	faire des commissions

_____   _____
_____   _____
_____   _____
_____   _____
_____   _____

to	**sack** (from job)	renvoyer
	sad	triste
	sail	la voile
	salad	la salade
on	**sale**	en vente
	salesperson	le vendeur/la vendeuse
	salmon	le saumon
	salt	le sel
the	**same thing**	la même chose
	sand	le sable
	sandal	la sandale
	sandwich	le sandwich
	sardine	la sardine
	satisfied	satisfait
	saucepan	la casserole
	saucer	la soucoupe
	sausage (not pre-cooked)	la saucisse
	sausage (pre-cooked)	le saucisson
to	**save**	sauver
to	**save** (money)	économiser
to	**say**	dire
	scarcely	à peine
	scarf (lady's)	l'écharpe (f)
	school	l'école (f)
	school (secondary)	le lycée
	science	la science
	scissors	les ciseaux (m)
	scooter	le scooter
	Scottish/Scotland	écossais/l'Ecosse (f)
	screen	l'écran (m)

sea	la mer
seafood	les fruits de mer (*m*)
seasickness	le mal de mer
season (of the year)	la saison
seat-belt	la ceinture de sécurité
second	deuxième
secretary	le/la secrétaire
section	la section
to see	voir
See you soon!	À bientôt! À tout à l'heure!
See you tomorrow!	À demain!
to seem	avoir l'air; paraître; sembler
to seize	saisir
to sell	vendre
to send	envoyer
sentence	la phrase
separated	séparé
serious	grave; sérieux (*m*)/ -ieuse (*f*)
to serve	servir
at your service	à votre service
service (not) included	service (non) compris
service station	la station-service
to set off	se mettre en route
to settle (e.g. in a chair)	s'installer
several	plusieurs
to sew	coudre

	sewing-machine	la machine à coudre
	sex	le sexe
	shadow	l'ombre (f)
to	shake hands	serrer la main
	shampoo	le shampooing
	shape	la forme
to	share	partager
	sharp	aigu (m)/aiguë (f)
to	shave	se raser
	sheep	le mouton
	sheet	le drap
	shelf	l'étagère (f)
	shelter	l'abri (m)
	ship	le navire
	shirt	la chemise
	shoe	la chaussure; le soulier
	shop	la boutique; le magasin
	shopping	les provisions (f)
	shop window	la vitrine
pair of		
	shorts	le short
	shoulder	l'épaule (f)
to	shout	crier
to	show	montrer
	show (entertainment)	le spectacle
	shower	la douche
	shower (of rain)	l'averse (f)
	shutter (on window)	le volet
	shy	timide

	sick	malade
	sideboard	le buffet
to	sigh	soupirer
to	sign	signer
	signature	la signature
	silence	le silence
	silk	la soie
	similar	pareil (*m*)/-eille (*f*)
	simple	simple
	since (with time)	depuis
	since (because)	puisque
to	sing	chanter
	singer	le chanteur/la chanteuse
	single (not married)	célibataire
	single ticket	l'aller simple (*m*)
	sink (for washing)	le bac; l'évier (*m*)
	sister	la sœur
to	sit down	s'asseoir
	situated	situé
	situation	la situation
	size (shoe, etc)	la pointure
to	skate	patiner
	skin	la peau
	skirt	la jupe
	sky	le ciel
to	sleep	dormir
	sleep	le sommeil
	sleeping bag	le sac de couchage
	sleeping car (on train)	le wagon-lit
to be	sleepy	avoir sommeil

slice	la tranche
slim	mince
to slip	glisser
slipper	la pantoufle
slow	lent
to slow down	ralentir
slowly	lentement
smart (i.e. well-dressed)	élégant
smell	l'odeur (f)
smile	le sourire
to smile	sourire
smoke	la fumée
to smoke	fumer
snail	l'escargot (m)
snake	le serpent
snow	la neige
to snow	neiger
so (happy)	si; tellement (content)
so (therefore)	donc
so much; so many	tant
So much the worse!	Tant pis!
to soak	tremper
soap	le savon
social	social
sock	la chaussette
socket (electrical)	la prise de courant
sofa	le canapé
soldier	le soldat
solid	solide
solution	la solution

someone	quelqu'un
something	quelque chose
sometimes	quelquefois
somewhere	quelque part
son	le fils
song	la chanson
soon	bientôt
sort	la sorte
sound	le son
to sound the horn	klaxonner
soup	le potage; la soupe
the south	le sud
the South of France	le Midi
Spanish/Spain	espagnol/l'Espagne (f)
spare time	les loisirs (m)
spare wheel	la roue de secours
to speak	parler
speciality	la spécialité
speed	la vitesse
to spell	épeler
to spend	dépenser
spinach	les épinards (m)
spiteful	méchant
to spoil	abîmer
sponge	l'éponge (f)
spoon	la cuiller/cuillère
sport	le sport
sporting	sportif (m)/-ive (f)
spring (season)	le printemps
square (shape)	carré

square (in a town)	la place
stadium	le stade
stain	la tache
stairs	l'escalier (*m*)
stamp	le timbre
to stamp (a ticket)	composter
standing	debout
star (in the sky)	l'étoile (*f*)
star (e.g. of a film)	la vedette
to start (e.g. a car)	démarrer
to start again	recommencer
starter (in a restaurant)	l'hors d'œuvre (*m*)
station	la gare
station (underground)	la station
stay	le séjour
to stay	rester
steak	le bifteck; le steak
to steal (something)	voler (quelquechose)
steamship	le vapeur
steering wheel	le volant
to stick	coller
still	toujours; encore
sting	la piqûre
to stir (coffee, etc)	remuer
stomach	l'estomac (*m*)
stomach-ache	le mal au ventre
stone	la pierre
stool	le tabouret
to stop	s'arrêter
to stop (doing something)	cesser de
storm	la tempête; l'orage (*m*)

stormy	orageux (*m*)/-euse (*f*)
stove	le poêle
stove (e.g. for camping)	le réchaud
straight on	tout droit
strange	bizarre
strawberry	la fraise
stream	le ruisseau
street	la rue
strict	sévère
strike (stopping work)	la grève
strong	fort
to **struggle**	lutter
stubborn	têtu
student	l'étudiant (*m*)/ l'étudiante (*f*)
studies	les études (*f*)
studio	l'atelier (*m*)
to **study**	étudier
subtitle	le sous-titre
subject (at school)	la matière
subscriber	l'abonné (*m*)/ l'abonnée (*f*)
subscription (to a club)	la cotisation
suburb	la banlieue; le faubourg
to **succeed**	réussir
such	tel (*m*)/telle (*f*)
sudden	soudain
suddenly	soudain; tout à coup
to **suffer**	souffrir
sugar	le sucre

to **suggest**	proposer; suggérer
suit	le costume
suitcase	la valise
sum (of money)	la somme
summer	l'été (*m*)
summit (of mountain)	le sommet
sun	le soleil
sunny	ensoleillé
sunstroke	le coup de soleil; l'insolation (*f*)
to **suntan**	se bronzer
supermarket	le supermarché
supplement	le supplément
to **supply**	fournir
to **suppose**	supposer
sure	sûr
surprising	surprenant
surrounded by	entouré de
to **suspect**	soupçonner
to **swallow**	avaler
to **swear**	jurer
sweater	le chandail
to **sweep**	balayer
sweet (e.g. for children)	le bonbon
sweet	doux (*m*)/douce (*f*)
to **swim**	nager
swimming	la natation
swimming pool	la piscine
Swiss/Switzerland	suisse/la Suisse
swollen	gonflé

table	la table
tablecloth	la nappe
table tennis	le ping-pong
tablet	le comprimé
tail (of animal)	la queue
to take	prendre
to take (a person)	emmener
to take advantage of	profiter
to take away	emporter
to take part in	participer
to take place	avoir lieu
tap	le robinet
tape recorder	le magnétophone
tart	la tarte
task	la tâche
taste	le goût
to taste	goûter
tax	la taxe; l'impôt (m)
tea	le thé
teapot	la théière
to teach	enseigner
teacher (secondary)	le/la professeur
teacher (primary)	l'instituteur (m)/ -trice (f)
team	l'équipe (f)
to tear	déchirer
telegram	le télégramme
telephone	le téléphone
to telephone	téléphoner
telephone call	le coup de téléphone
telephone directory	l'annuaire (m)

telephone box	la cabine téléphonique
television	la télévision
television set	le téléviseur; le récepteur
to tell (someone)	dire
to tell (e.g. a story)	raconter
temperature	la température
temperature (when ill)	la fièvre
temporary	temporaire
ten (approx.)	une dizaine
tennis	le tennis
tent	la tente
term (e.g. at school)	le trimestre
terrible	terrible
to thank	remercier
thanks to	grâce à
thank you	merci
that is to say	c'est-à-dire
theatre	le théâtre
theft	le vol
their	leur
them	eux
then	alors; ensuite; puis
there	là; y
there is; there are	il y a; voilà
thick	épais (*m*)/épaisse (*f*)
thief	le voleur
thin	maigre
thing	la chose
to think	penser; réfléchir
thirst	la soif

to be **thirsty**	avoir soif
this	ce/cet/cette
this way	par ici
(a) **thousand**	mille (*m*)
to **threaten**	menacer
throat	la gorge
through	par
to **throw**	jeter; lancer
thunder	le tonnerre
ticket	le billet
ticket office	le guichet
to **tidy** (e.g. a room)	ranger
tie (that you wear)	la cravate
tights	les collants (*m*)
at what **time?**	à quelle heure?
from **time** to time	de temps en temps
on **time**	à l'heure
timetable (at a station)	l'horaire (*m*)
timetable (in a school)	l'emploi du temps (*m*)
tin-opener	l'ouvre-boîtes (*m*)
tip (e.g. to a waitress)	le pourboire
tired	fatigué
title	le titre
tobacco	le tabac
today	aujourd'hui
toe	l'orteil (*m*)
together	ensemble
toilet-block	le bloc sanitaire
toilets	les toilettes (*f*); les W.C. (*m*)

token (for using phone)	le jeton
toll	le péage
tomato	la tomate
tomorrow	demain
tone (on phone)	la tonalité
tongue	la langue
too	trop
tool	l'outil (*m*)
tooth	la dent
toothache	mal (*m*) aux dents
toothpaste	le dentifrice; la pâte dentifrice
tortoise	la tortue
to **touch**	toucher
tourism	le tourisme
tourist	le/la touriste
towards	vers
towel	l'essuie-mains (*m*); la serviette
tower	la tour
town	la ville
town hall	la mairie; l'hôtel de ville (*m*)
toy	le jouet
track (at station)	la voie
tradesman	le commerçant
traffic	la circulation
give way to **traffic from right**	priorité à droite
traffic jam	l'embouteillage (*m*)
traffic light	le feu rouge

train	le train
transistor	le transistor
to translate	traduire
to travel	voyager
travel agency	l'agence de voyages (*f*)
traveller	le voyageur
traveller's cheque	le chèque de voyage
tray	le plateau
tree	l'arbre (*m*)
to tremble	trembler
to trim	tailler
trolley (supermarket)	le chariot
trousers	le pantalon
trout	la truite
true	vrai
truly	vraiment
truth	la vérité
to try	essayer
tube	le tube
to turn	tourner
twin	le jumeau/la jumelle
twinning (of towns)	le jumelage
to twist	tordre
type	l'espèce (*f*)
typewriter	la machine à écrire
typical	typique
typist	le/la dactylographe
tyre	le pneu

ugly	laid
umbrella	le parapluie
unbearable	insupportable
uncle	l'oncle (*m*)
under	sous
the **underground** (trains)	le métro
underpants	le slip
to **understand**	comprendre
to **undress**	se déshabiller
undubbed (film)	version originale
unemployment	le chômage
unfortunately	malheureusement
unhappy	malheureux (*m*)/ -euse (*f*)
uniform	l'uniforme (*m*)
unique	unique
the **United Kingdom**	le Royaume-Uni
the **United States**	les Etats-Unis (*m*)
university	l'université (*f*)
unknown	inconnu
unpleasant	désagréable
until	jusqu'à
unusual	rare
upper	supérieur
to **upset**	bouleverser
upstairs	en haut
urgent	urgent
to **use**	employer; se servir de; utiliser
useful	pratique; utile
useless	inutile

usherette	l'ouvreuse (*f*)
usually	d'habitude

_____   _____
_____   _____
_____   _____
_____   _____
_____   _____

ABCDEFGHIJKLMNOPQRSTU**V**WXYZ

vacuum-cleaner	l'aspirateur (*m*)
valid (e.g. a ticket)	valable
valley	la vallée
value	la valeur
van	la camionnette
vanilla	la vanille
to vary	varier
vase	le vase
vegetable	le légume
vehicle	le véhicule
veil (e.g. over face)	le voile
version	la version
very	très
very sorry	désolé
video recorder	le magnétoscope
view (over the sea)	la vue (sur la mer)
village	le village
vine	la vigne

vinegar	le vinaigre
vineyard	le vignoble
violence	la violence
violin	le violon
visibility	la visibilité
visit	la visite
to visit	visiter
visitor	le visiteur/la visiteuse
voice	la voix
to vomit	vomir

_____   _____
_____   _____
_____   _____
_____   _____

ABCDEFGHIJKLMNOPQRSTUV**W**XYZ

wage	le salaire
waist	la taille
to wait for	attendre
waiter (in a café)	le garçon
waiting-room	la salle d'attente
to wake up	se réveiller
Wales	le Pays de Galles
to walk	marcher
walk	la promenade
wall	le mur

wallet	le portefeuille
to want	désirer; vouloir
to want to	avoir envie de
war	la guerre
wardrobe	l'armoire (f)
to wash yourself	se laver
washbasin	le lavabo
to do the washing	faire la lessive
washing-machine	la machine à laver
to do the washing-up	faire la vaisselle
water	l'eau (f)
to water	arroser
wave	la vague
weak	faible
to wear (clothes)	porter (des vêtements)
weather forecast	la météo
week	la semaine
weekend	le week-end
weight	le poids
welcome	l'accueil (m)
Welcome!	Bienvenue!
to welcome	accueillir
welcome	bienvenu
Well, well!	Tiens!
well-behaved	sage
Welsh	gallois
the west	l'ouest (m)
western (film)	le western

wet	mouillé
wheel	la roue
when	quand; lorsque
where	où
whereas	tandis que
which?	quel (*m*)/quelle (*f*)?
while	pendant que
to whistle	siffler
white	blanc (*m*)/blanche (*f*)
whose	dont
why?	pourquoi?
wide	large
widow	la veuve
widower	le veuf
wife	l'épouse (*f*); la femme
willingly	volontiers
wind	le vent
window	la fenêtre
windowpane	la vitre
windscreen	le pare-brise
wine	le vin
winter	l'hiver (*m*)
winter sport	le sport d'hiver
to wipe	essuyer
to wish	souhaiter; vouloir
All good wishes!	Tous mes voeux!
with	avec
without	sans

witness	le témoin
woman	la femme
wood	le bois
wool	la laine
word	le mot; la parole
work	le travail
to work	travailler
worker	l'ouvrier (*m*)/ l'ouvrière (*f*)
works	les travaux (*m*)
workshop	l'atelier (*m*)
worm	le ver
worn-out	usé
worried	inquiet (*m*)/inquiète (*f*)
to worry	s'inquiéter
worry	le souci
worse	pire
it is worth while	il vaut la peine
wrist	le poignet
to write	écrire
writing paper	le papier à lettres
to be wrong	avoir tort

_____   _____
_____   _____
_____   _____
_____   _____
_____   _____

year	un an (*m*); une année (*f*)
yellow	jaune
yes	oui
yes (after a negative)	si
yesterday	hier
yogurt	le yaourt
young	jeune
younger	cadet (*m*)/cadette (*f*)
youth	la jeunesse
youth club	la maison des jeunes
youth hostel	l'auberge de jeunesse (*f*)

ABCDEFGHIJKLMNOPQRSTUVWXY**Z**

zone	la zone
zoo	le zoo